"I love you and I have dreams. . . . I think I'd be willing to do just about anything if I felt it would bring us together again. . . . I'm really missing you. No one to eat with. No one to talk and pray with. No human warmth, especially at night. . . . Come home, beloved Bonnie".—Randy

"You can't imagine the mess we have now with property, with taxes, with mortgage payments, with children's support, and layoffs. It blows my mind. Between a husband who acts as if you don't exist, and three teenage children, you can lose your identity pretty fast. . . . To be stood up to such an existence spells failure in life. . . . It's hard just to stay alive!" —Kate

"Mom tried to kill herself before Dad left. He scolded her severely. A minister's wife isn't supposed to do things like that. . . . She felt left out of his life. He was gone so much. . . . Mother's resentment began to show through more and more. Especially when she learned why father was away from home so much. There was another woman."—A young nurse.

"For years I felt like a machine that one can put a quarter in and get out something that meets needs and desires. A 'sex machine' I guess you'd call it. . . . . Many times my husband didn't bother to put the quarter in. He just expected me to operate. Pretty soon I felt like a Raggedy Ann sexually. So the divorce—why not? What else would you expect?"—Gail

"I'm not married, and I'm not a man. . . but I think the Lord is prompting me to say something. . . . We've been hearing a lot about women's lib and about how men have been treating women as sex objects. But during the past several weeks I've come to realize that I'm doing the same thing with men—except in a little more subtle way. . . . With the Lord's help I'm trying to change my way of thinking. . . . I just don't want illicit sex in my life."—From a church discussion group participant.

DIVORCE
A Christian Dilemma

Norma Martin
and Zola Levitt

Introduction by
John R. Martin

HERALD PRESS
Scottdale, Pennsylvania
Kitchener, Ontario

DIVORCE, A CHRISTIAN DILEMMA
Copyright © 1977 by Herald Press, Scottdale, Pa. 15683
  Published simultaneously in Canada by Herald Press,
  Kitchener, Ont. N2G 4M5
Library of Congress Catalog Card Number: 76-45939
International Standard Book Number: 0-8361-1808-1
Printed in the United States of America
Design: Alice B. Shetler

10 9 8 7 6 5 4 3 2

To those who shared
their dilemma
to help
other marriages survive.

CONTENTS

INTRODUCTION

Few ethical issues are more critical for the church today than the issue of divorce and remarriage. The issue is critical in depth—the sanctity of Christian marriage is at stake. The issue is critical in scope—most congregations are seeking God's direction.

Numerous authors are speaking to the issue. New books on the subject are on the increase. *Divorce, A Christian Dilemma* is not just another book on divorce and remarriage. It is different in its approach and unique in its message.

The dilemma of the Christian divorcee is usually discussed either from the perspective of theology with little concern for human hurt, or from the perspective of human hurt with little concern for theology. Norma Martin and Zola Levitt combine both perspectives. They bring together the life stories of those caught in marriage failure along with solid teaching by serious biblical scholars. This book will prove profitable for all committed people of compassion.

Those who have not felt the human agony of marriage failure will be moved by the true experiences recorded by Norma Martin in the early chapters of this book. She presents heart-rending slices of life that all caring Christians need to encounter. Divorced persons are not merely problems, they are people. Our hearts should ache with those whose hearts and lives have been broken.

Those who seek a deeper understanding of the theology of marriage will profit by the illuminating discussion by Paul Miller in chapter 5. "The coming together of man and woman achieves the same oneness that Adam possessed before Eve was taken from his side." What a lofty concept! Miller sees the marriage vows or covenant as the essence of marriage. Divorce then becomes an act of covenant breaking. As a counselor, Miller points out that sex cannot be disassociated from committed relationships. Sexual relations outside of marriage leads to the disintegration of personality.

Those who would ignore the teachings of Jesus on divorce and remarriage and those who ignore the reality of forgiveness will benefit from the provocative comments of Howard Charles in chapter 6. Charles stresses both the warning of the gospel to those who take divorce lightly and the forgiveness of the gospel to those who will face its sinfulness.

Those who wrestle with the temptation of adultery—whether single, married, or divorced—find help through the insights of Ray Bair and his congregational study group. Holiness is both a position in Christ and a walk with Christ. We all walk with feet of clay in bodies of flesh. But these bodies can be energized by God

Himself. Therein hope and victory is possible.

Those who have never grasped the analogy between the Jewish marriage pattern and the teachings of Jesus about us, the church, will gain new perspective from the exciting love story by Zola Levitt (chapter 8). Did you know that the Christian is "engaged to Christ" awaiting a divine marriage? What a fitting perspective for those of us who struggle with the tragedies and perplexities of life.

Norma Martin and Zola Levitt are to be commended for their competent and sensitive handling of a complex issue. Out of their efforts has come a creative book, an enlightening message for the Christian church.

August 9, 1976   *John R. Martin*
                                        Harrisonburg, Virginia

AUTHOR'S PREFACE

"I wear a label on my back, D-I-V-O-R-C-E-E. It's a *disease* to me. I'd rather be dead!" she blurted out to me as she cried convulsively.

I wept.

Divorce with dignity? Is it ever a satisfactory solution? Is it a permissible option for Christians with a problem marriage?

When Christians face such a crisis, where can they go? Will they find caring and concern in community health centers? In the counselor's office? The church? Where can they turn?

I searched for answers. I went to churches that were studying the divorce issue. I interviewed the people who were the victims of the studies. I arrived on the scene to find many emotional tragedies, relational deaths, and "just a matter of time" situations.

I realized no one owned an effective marriage-preservation kit that "worked." I wondered who might have one. My not-involved-in-the-tragedies friends also wondered.

Dr. Daniel M. McGann, a well-to-do unbeliever who had a "mind of Christ" transformation, expressed grave concern to me one day at our Bible study in his home that so many of his friends are caught in the divorce dilemma. He said a book should be written about these people, and for these people.° He was sure the church would be the caring community to help heal sick marriages.

I went to these people. I went to groups. I went to churches to see if the church was the caring community. The pages that follow reveal the exposed, raw feelings I discovered as well as some of the theological considerations I encountered. (Names and details have been altered when necessary to mask the identity of those involved.)

Zola Levitt, a mutual friend of Dan and mine, did the final writing—gently and tenderly because of his not-vicarious involvement.

Zola and I wish to thank John R. Martin (author of *Divorce and Remarriage: A Perspective for Counseling*, Herald Press, 1974 and 1976), Paul M. Miller, Howard H. Charles, Ray Bair, and Maggie Glick for reading the manuscript and suggesting improvements. We also acknowledge the Man of Sorrows whose own acquaintance with grief has made Him able to become the Shepherd who restoreth. . . .

July 23, 1976
                              Norma F. Martin
                              Fort Wayne, Indiana

°Dr. McGann coauthored two books as a new convert with Zola Levitt—*How Did a Fat Balding Middle-aged Jew Like You Become a Jesus Freak?* Tyndale House, 1974, and *Christ in the Country Club*, Herald Press, 1976.

1
"Come Home, Beloved Bonnie"

My very special and precious Bonnie,

Honey, please, as you read this be fair with me and don't be too hard on me. I would rather share as we used to and hear both sides, and then be able to pray aloud together. Since that doesn't seem to be possible, I will use this method and pray that you understand.

When I remember what our home meant to me, and I think to you also, I have to wonder if you have considered the condition of our home these past three weeks. I never wanted it this way.

Being without you isn't easy. I am suffering. I pray no permanent damage has come to either of us. I always thought we thought of ourselves as partners. Partners together for each other, and for God and His service.

Our months together weren't really all that bad, were they?

I love you, and I have dreams. I want to be a companion to you and I want you to be my companion as I believe He plans. I just can't shake this idea. I guess God just doesn't want me to and won't let me shake it. I think I'd be willing to do just about anything if I felt it would help bring us together again. You are the only person I have ever loved. Oh, honey, I love you so much and I wish I could tell you often, whenever I wanted to.

Come home, beloved Bonnie.

I'm really missing you. No one to eat with. No one to talk and pray with. No human warmth, especially at night. And mostly I'm missing just the presence of you—the very touch and nearness and warmth of your human being—your own special one.

Honey, I love you so very much.

Alone,
Randy

* * *

It didn't work. Bonnie returned Randy's letter unopened.

The separation had started when Randy returned from work one day to find his wife and baby and the baby's crib gone. Bonnie had simply taken little Rodney and left. There was no good-bye, no forwarding address. She couldn't have gone far, Randy knew, since she had no money. But she was gone, and she left a real vacancy.

Randy was terribly uneasy because Bonnie was obviously emotionally upset. She might go off the deep end. They had fought. She was depressed. Where *was* she, and where was the baby?

A sympathetic friend finally confided to Randy

that his wife and baby were living in a flophouse at the other end of their town! And Bonnie *had* been going off the deep end. She was up to no good in that place. The friend advised Randy that the situation needed some looking into.

Randy went down to the unsavory "week's-rent-in-advance" rooming house to find his wife. She saw him for only a few minutes—enough time to make clear that she wasn't coming back. She and the baby would go it alone, she said.

The place was filthy, and possibly dangerous. Maybe it would provide for some baser instinct in Bonnie, but it wasn't fair to an infant. Rodney deserved better. But how could Randy rescue his son at least?

He took the question to a lawyer.

Randy obtained a court order to take Rodney back with him, out of that place. Bonnie could do as she pleased, but she could not keep Rodney with her. She could come back to her husband, remain separated, get a divorce, or whatever. But she could not have her baby and her chosen new life together.

Randy took his mother along when he went back to the rooming house with the court order. He said it was so that she could hold Rodney while he drove home. Maybe it was for emotional support. Few people would choose to undertake such a mission alone.

The operator of the place didn't like the situation too well, but he let Randy in when he showed the court order. Randy and his mother found Rodney lying in the corner of a smelly room sucking on a bottle of soured milk. He was whimpering. His diaper hadn't been changed for a long time. The milk bottle was all he had; it was sustenance for him, such as it was, and his lone toy. He was living a grim existence for a 5-month old, by the looks of things. Bonnie was nowhere to be found.

Well and good, thought Randy, as he grabbed up his son and fled.

Both Randy and his mother had to stop shaking before they could drive away from the place. The baby was dazed. They went directly to Randy's parents' home, to try to sort things out.

For awhile Randy and the baby lived alone. But when Randy saw that Bonnie would not ever be coming back, he gave up their place and moved in with his parents. Rodney would at least have a grandmother around, if not a mother.

Life went on, as it will. It became clear after a while that Bonnie had no further interest in her husband or son and seemed instead to be going all out to provide grounds for a divorce. Jesus mentioned adultery in that connection, and Bonnie was gaining a reputation for it. It seemed as though a divorce was inevitable, though it left Randy spiritually confused. Sometimes he wondered what part he had played in causing Bonnie to react as she had. The whole affair left him puzzled, bewildered, and numb.

His friends at church knew Randy was a sensitive, thinking man. He was tall and spare, with a mod moustache and sandy, unruly hair, and he seemed to enjoy his own thoughts more than the conversation of others. He believed deeply in God and took his churchgoing seriously. He believed that Christian people should not divorce.

But Bonnie had quickly found another liaison, and in a matter of weeks she was demanding the right to remarry. The divorce was granted easily, in terms of the legal aspects. Bonnie remarried immediately and Randy and Rodney went on as they were.

Available women in Randy's town noticed how eligible he was as time went on. They took to phoning him since he showed no inclination to pursue a romantic life. It wasn't that he hated women now or had been made gun-shy by his experience; he was simply examining his spiritual life with great care. Specifically, he was participating in a church group which was undertaking an intensive study of divorce and remarriage.

It was a new church for Randy because he preferred to go where his special need might be met. Underlying his calm exterior and his surface reserve toward women was a driving interest in remarriage, if it were possible. Randy was a young man, and very lonely.

He met Gretchen at the church where they were studying divorce and remarriage, and she was there for the same purposes. Soon after Bonnie had left him, Randy began leaning on Gretchen. In the period while he still kept house with Rodney, before he moved in with his parents, Gretchen had been a great help. Unlike the other women of the local community who had seemed to close in like vultures, Gretchen had perceived the depth of Randy's despair. She didn't talk a lot about romantic matters, she just went ahead with some of the cooking and cleaning around the place so that Rodney's father might have more time with him.

They fell in love. And that became quite a problem.

In a way, Randy had based all his hopes for a good life on *not* falling in love. He'd had an interview with his pastor at the crucial moment when Bonnie had left and the pastor made his point all too clearly. Divorce was out. God hated divorce. Divorce is a loophole man used to alter God's plans and principles for an orderly spiritual life. Divorce destroys what God intended to be holy. Moses permitted divorce only because men's hearts had turned hard, but Christians must never imitate the hardhearted. Jesus restated the fact that Moses permitted divorce, but Jesus never gave consent Himself.

Randy left his church. He felt condemned.

His life of zero-love was livable until Gretchen. And now he had the very real problem of loving a woman who loved him back, and loving a God who, according to some, did not approve.

Loving Gretchen felt wonderful, but being condemned felt horrible. And his divorce was only half the problem. He incurred much disapproval in various sectors of the Christian community for being divorced. But the *real* difficulties would lie ahead—if he attempted to remarry.

In that spirit he attended the church studies, sitting beside Gretchen and remaining in prayer.

At length Randy and Gretchen consulted with *her* pastor. Here, after all, was a pastor who condoned at least the study of the problem in his church. Could they, conceivably, be the guinea pigs for the discussions? Would the church groups who were studying marriage and divorce consider a real-life case? Would it provide useful input to have flesh and blood people on the scene whose love for each other was obvious?

In short, would the church consider whether Randy and Gretchen might marry?

It was touchy.

The morality of the entire human community is amazingly diversified. In some sectors of even the local society Randy and Gretchen could have married in a minute. Indeed, they would never have considered what other people thought—at least among unbelievers. At any secular university these days they could live together with impunity among their fellows without even going through the motions of a marriage ceremony. But here, at the spiritual end of society—which they preferred, of course—there was serious question about them even *thinking* about marriage. Some no doubt felt that they ought not even keep company.

The church took on the challenge. Randy told them in a general meeting that he would abide by what they decided and would harbor no hard feelings if they said no.

The church tackled the problem with enthusiasm, even calling in special resource people to guide their discussion groups. Question-answer sessions were held under the guidance of the resource people and the entire sticky area of divorce and remarriage was scrutinized carefully.

Randy and Gretchen had a secret confidence

that the matter would come out in their favor, and it brought them closer together. They even chose a certain month in which they wanted to get married, and they prayed that the church would reach a positive conclusion before that month.

The courtship was touchy too. The two rather public lovers spent little time alone together. The "waiting period" was artificial and it placed a strain on the relationship. The biblical admonishments against incontinence were constantly in the minds of Randy and Gretchen whose mutual desire for each other continued to grow. Randy studiously kept to public places with his partner, not trusting himself to avoid the temptations that awaited them with every glance at each other.

The secret month of decision came and went.

The church hadn't made much progress. The resource people contradicted each other. Sometimes the same person would say seemingly opposite things. Randy recalled one leader who stated that an individual who honestly tried for reconciliation of a marriage and failed was free to remarry. Then the same commentator went on to say that the individual would be living in continuous sin if he did remarry.

Randy and Gretchen tried seeing each other less to take the stress out of the situation for a while. It did have that effect. In fact, they grew somewhat distant as the church went on with the discussions over the better part of a year.

One night Randy just failed to show up at the meeting. It was easier that way.

He never went back.

And he allowed the relationship with Gretchen to slip away. It seemed in a way that their love for each other was so great, and their communication so precise, that they both realized that a total sacrifice was better than an ongoing frustration. They had, in a way, brought each other grief. They now spared each other more pain. By staying apart, regardless of the effort that took, they slowly quenched their love.

Randy today is very frustrated. He is not a man of many words, but the few he is willing to express sum up his situation—a situation occurring all too often in the twentieth-century church. He says he feels empty, alone, and alienated. He wonders how he can continue "chaste, celibate, and a hermit," as he puts it. He says, "I believe the theology about divorce. But now we need a theology about loneliness—about pain."

o o o

Gail was married and divorced before she really knew what a woman was. And she happened to marry a man equally ignorant of that subject.

She makes no bones about the reason for her divorce, and gives no apologies, spiritual or otherwise. She did not really make contact with God until after her divorce. She was caught in a very unhappy marriage and she terminated it. And that's all there was to that.

She had a lot to learn.

At the first social gathering Gail went to following her divorce she was propositioned by five men. They were the husbands of her five best friends. They were churchgoing "brothers," but one could hardly say "God-fearing."

Gail realized that she needed help. She turned to the Lord.

*　*　*

Mary Jane's very appearance suggested her dread fear of remarriage. She was painfully thin, pale as a porcelain doll, and she trembled as she read the Bible. The Sermon on the Mount was for her the pronouncements of an Executioner. She'd been divorced twice.

"But I'm just the kind of person who needs a man badly," she confessed to her church study group, on the verge of tears. She garnered a hesitant sympathy.

"What are the chances of my making a go of a third marriage?" she asked them. Nobody really wanted to give an estimate.

*　*　*

Helen wasn't left alone after her divorce. She was left with her five young children. She had only one night a week which she reserved to leave the house.

She spent it with her church group, studying divorce and remarriage.

*　*　*

Caroline was 49 and she was attending the study group on behalf of her son. She herself was happily married, but her oldest child had divorced his wife.

"You're not going to tell me that because my

son made a mistake in choosing a bride when he was only a youngster that he's going to be denied sex for the rest of his life, are you?" she queried. "I mean, if he lives a continent Christian life and he can't remarry, what is he supposed to do with what God provided? The boy is only 23!"

o   o   o

A young fellow named Dan told his church, "If I were poor or black or a foreigner, you'd all accept me. Well, I happen to be divorced. Why can't you accept my "disability"?

o   o   o

Rosie was having an extremely tough time. She was 60. She'd been married 40 years. Now she was divorced.

When her husband left, he'd taken her world with him. He'd even taken their savings account. She needed work to live, but she couldn't work. She couldn't even think straight.

She spent ten weeks in the local hospital's psychiatric unit, but it wasn't clear whether she was going to bounce back from the shock or not. It's hard to fix an old machine.

Sympathy was not enough. The church would have had to look far to find anyone with even vaguely the same problem. Her friends were accustomed to experiencing her as one-half of an established couple. Now they avoided her as if she had contracted a disease—or, as if what she had contracted were contagious. Her women friends had a dread fear of even hearing the details. Men looked the other way.

Nobody needed her, and nobody particularly wanted her. She'd gone to God's house, knowing that God would not forsake her, but she'd found the members of the church stymied by her situation.

Only God Himself would understand, she felt, and she made those about her very uneasy with her constant wish to go directly to Him, by means of an early death.

2

"Cry for Me, Norma!"

Coauthor Norma Martin did not have to travel far to gather those stories about the hell on earth called divorce. She discovered them all within the area where she lived.

Among her troubled interviewees she found one who presented some grim realities from her reading. The divorce rate has exceeded the marriage rate in the United States. A concept of "no-fault divorce" is gaining support in which no lawyer is needed, the divorce costs are nil, there is no dispute over property, child custody, or alimony, and the proceedings can be finalized within six weeks, or less. Worldwide, divorce in the 20-to-24-year-old group has increased nearly 40 percent in the past fifteen years.

Those trends affect the entirety of our society, including the Christian church. Apparently even some Bible believers, strictly admonished in the Scriptures against divorce, are among those unhappy statistics. Many churches can report divorced men and women among their membership these days (or no longer among their membership) and many a pastor wrestles constantly with this encroaching threat against the sanctity of Christian marriage. (But interestingly, Billy Graham reports that only one divorce in every 450 marriages takes place in homes where the Bible is read regularly.)

This book is an attempt to shine some light into what have long been dark corners. Divorce has long had a stigma attached to it and has not been a popular topic for public discussion. The feelings and needs of the divorced have not enjoyed a great deal of attention in the church.

Norma Martin is not a marriage counselor or a theologian but she is a Christian of compassion. In her role as a nurse she has heard many confessions of one sort or another; people seem to unburden themselves more readily when they are ill. In her role as a disciple of Christ she has become aware of people in spiritual pain. That pain grows intense in the divorce situation. Norma has responded by thoroughly investigating the area, counseling as she could those in need, and arduously collecting the personal interviews and scholarly information included in this book.

We have given, in rather brief form, some of the agony of divorce in the preceding section. We will continue in this chapter with actual divorce cases, this time recorded as much as possible in the exact words of the persons involved. Norma went first to the sources of the pain, the hearts of the participants in divorce, and patiently recorded what are usually secrets in the Christian community. Names and details have been changed in deference to the feelings of those involved.

Stanley left his wife, Kate, and their three sons after 20 years of marriage. He also left the church, where he had been participating with Kate in one of those marriage studies. It became common knowledge after the divorce that Stanley had been seeing another woman in the community for some time, and he married her immediately after the divorce was final. He lived with her during the waiting period, and this was known to his three teenagers.

Kate poured out her story in a five-hour discourse with Norma Martin, the tape recorder running. The following are excerpts from her highly-charged report of all that happened:

There was something the matter between Stanley and me and I just didn't know what. I could tell that things just weren't right. I wanted closeness and there just wasn't any. And the more I wanted it, the more things I did to make him go away, it seemed.

Whenever we would get into a fight he would become very angry, and I'd more than likely pout, which didn't make him feel any better either.

Then we went to this birthday party together. It was on the way home from the party that he just said, "You ought to see a lawyer and file for divorce." Just like that!

And I said, "I don't . . . I don't . . . I'm not . . . I don't want to file for a divorce." He said, "Well, you might as well. I did."

And I said, "You did what!" He said, "I filed for divorce today." All I could say was, "How come?" He said, "Incompatability."

When we got home I just sat out in the car for a while. I couldn't go in. He went into the house and I just . . . everything was moving so fast . . . I just . . . I just couldn't get myself together.

Finally I went in and started doing some stuff in the kitchen. He and the boys were just sitting there, and I said, "Stanley, don't you think you have something to tell the boys?"

The boys said, "Oh, we already know." He had told them before we went to the party! That made me mad!

I screamed and hollered and yelled and called him a snake in the grass. And he sat there like he was unconcerned. He had the situation well in hand. I was out of my cool. I was angry . . . fit to be tied. After I ranted for a while, with him just sitting there not reacting, I laid down on the bed and I cried for about half an hour.

Then I decided, "Well, I just can't stay in this house any longer," and I went out to the barn. I was out there for about half an hour and it was about 11:30 by that time. I thought, "I can't go back into the house. What am I going to do?"

I have a neighbor down here who is a very good listener. I knew they would be in bed but I decided I was going to go down there anyway. I got her out of bed and told her what had happened. She let me talk and talk and talk. From her kitchen window I could see up to the house, and all the lights were on. It was very late by that time.

My neighbor said, "Do you want to stay down here tonight?"

I told her, "I don't know what I want."

She said, "It looks like they're expecting you."

I thought, "Well, if Stanley's looking for me, let him look."

Then I decided that my children might be frightened and that I'd better put away some of my anger and my fear and think about them. So at that point I went back home.

Stanley then told me that he was planning to stay in the house with us until the divorce was final. You can do that in this state . . . you can both stay under the same roof. And that's what he wanted to do! The divorce is supposed to take two months, at the shortest, but ours took five.

After a while I couldn't stand him being in the house. I told him, "If you don't want to live here, would you just get out of here?" And I asked him if there was another woman and he said, "Well, there might be."

That's the way it always was . . . "there *might* be," "there *could* be" . . . always evasive. And whenever I'd mention it he would just hit the ever-lovin' ceiling.

Well, he left and I think he lived *there* . . . at her house . . . before they were married. Nobody told me that outright, but after he was out of here he took the boys where he was living. Now I've never asked them where they went, and they've never told me, but I also never heard of him moving twice. I mean, he just stayed where he was when they married.

I didn't know just when they got married. That's what really hurt all along . . . the deceptiveness, the not-talking; that treatment has

31

made it a lot worse than just a plain divorce. When he left I sent the boys to just ask for a phone number . . . you know, for an emergency or something . . . and he said, "She can always call the police."

Well, at this point I'm still *very* angry. Until you talk with . . . live with . . . *be with* someone in my situation, you have no idea what it's like.

Take last Sunday, for instance. Our church is working through divorce and remarriage—and I feel every church should work something through on it. Well, anyhow, I made the statement that as far as I'm able to see, there's no reason for me to remarry because Stanley is still living. I said I have such deep feelings against him that I could kill him. One lady came to me after the service and said, "I had no idea you feel that way." I guess I shocked her, but I don't see how you can go through divorce without being full of hate and anger.

Believe me, I don't care anymore about the way she thinks. I feel the way I feel. It just never occurred to me that people couldn't know how I feel. I didn't know until I went through this what divorce is all about or what it's like.

I would guess that if you interviewed Stanley, he'd have a completely different way of saying how he feels about the church. He pulled out. There are some people and things he could still identify with maybe. Some of the things the church downed him for are good, some are bad, and some are indifferent.

However I feel accepted as a divorced person in my church, because I stayed with the church; I didn't leave and get remarried. But I'll bet that if I stayed in this same church and got remarried, I'd not be accepted by the same people and the same church that accepts me now.

I want to trust these people because I feel they accept me now. But how soon will they not trust me? How many are watching me now to see if I have a boyfriend? How many already wonder what I'm doing with my time?

You see, the Bible says so and so. But I need *love*! So why should I stick with the church? I have a label on my back—Divorcee! I know a lot of people in the church who are *emotionally* divorced but have not gone through the courts. I carry the stigma; they do not. What's the real difference? Am I not being more honest? And yet, they may run me out of the church, or at least disapprove of what step I might take next. It gets to you after a while.

I've figured a few things out for myself. I will not have sex without marriage. And I will not marry if I don't love him—the man I'd marry and have sex with. Anyone hearing me talk about Stanley knows I'm still attached to him. As long as I am in love with Stanley, I feel safe from being sexually involved with anyone else. And I'm safe from having to decide if I will remarry. That is my safety at this point. There's no reason for me to go out there into that world I know nothing about—and have known nothing about for 20 years—while married to Stanley.

Furthermore, I don't want to go out there. It's scary! So as long as I'm married in my head, I don't need to go out and face what's there.

But, in reality, I'm single. Single for the first time. And that's *really* scary. I never was single. I got married right out of high school. I have no idea what the standards for being single are. I never was single.

Also, realistically, I know it's not good for me to stay emotionally attached to Stanley. As soon as I get unattached, I'll be free. But I don't know how to cope with being free. This new world with its new standards I'm to fit into is something that approximately 200,000 other couples will experience with me this year—couples that have been married for over fifteen years, that is. So I might as well get with it and put on my walking shoes. But I'd rather be dead!

I'll bet you can't imagine the mess we have now with property, with taxes, with mortgage payments, with children's support, and layoffs. It blows my mind.

Between a husband who acts as if you don't exist, and three teenage children, you can lose your identity pretty fast. You wonder if you *belong*, and to what or whom you belong. To be stood up to such an existence—which spells failure in life—is really a struggle for survival.

It's hard just to stay alive!

o   o   o

Hospital floors are usually pretty quiet at night. Norma sought the opportunity to interview a co-worker, a divorced nurse, the daughter of a minister. She got quite a story:

The scars I am sensing in my own life have come from my divorce. However my parents were divorced. And it may be that my scars are a result of that experience when I was a child. But I do know I have scars, real scars, that will last a lifetime.

There is so much going on at the time of a divorce that a child may not be able to understand the implications. For example, I thought my world had been destroyed when my parents were divorced. Something died in me. I was happy when my mother and father were both home and I could be where both were. My father was away a lot, he was a minister. But when I was told to choose whom I wanted to live with—my mother or my daddy—I went into some type of shock. I've never been the same since. I wanted both my father and mother. I didn't know they could be divided. I loved both. I wanted both. But I was told I couldn't have both. My world crumbled.

I don't know how to explain it to make myself understood, but my life, my security seemed like a balloon that had burst before me. I'd lie awake at nights and remember when I was ill. I recalled to myself how Mother took tender care of me. I knew I couldn't go on in life without that. I needed my mother. I couldn't choose to leave her. Then I would think about how my father and I had a special relationship. I felt I was his favorite over my brother. We simply understood each other so well. I couldn't choose to leave him. I needed him to understand me. I couldn't bear to think of being without him, just as much as I absolutely couldn't bear to think of being without my mother. How could I make a choice that would separate me from either? I couldn't. I believe some of my growth and development stopped at that point in my life.

I remember hearing the folks quarrel. It was awful, the accusations, the words. But I think I'd rather have heard the selfish, stubborn quarreling between them continue than to feel the loneliness and the despair. I would have gladly replaced my crushed broken heart for a few alive quarrels by my parents.

I also remember a note my brother wrote in school one day. It said "Dear Mother. Dear Daddy. I love you. I need you. I want you." It was all crumpled up in his pocket. I saw the bulge on our way home from school. I asked him what it was. He showed it to me. We both had felt a bit ignored that morning. I always felt deep tenderness for my brother. We were only one year apart. My grades were dropping. So were his. We were really knit together. We felt we had everything in common.

Mom tried to kill herself before Dad left. He scolded her severely. A minister's wife isn't supposed to do things like that, you know. Dad acted so uncaring about her, even though he was very kind and sweet to me. They were married young. Dad went to seminary. We children came along so soon. Everything must have been a struggle for them. Dad had to study hard as well as work at a job. Mother seemed not to be able to adjust to his busy schedule. She felt left out of his life. He was gone so much. Little attitudes trickled into her that she was not aware of. Dad sensed them though. So he began to stay away from home more than ever. When he was home, he devoted his time to us children. We loved it. We weren't really aware of the coolness between them spreading them apart as it was. Each of them was devoted to us—probably to make a buffer for us so that we would not feel the real effects of the negative vibrations.

But Mother's resentment began to show through more and more. Especially when she learned why our father was staying away from home so much. There was another woman. When the church got wind of it, they whisked him out the back door. And quick. There was an eventual divorce and Dad moved to another state. The other lady went along. They were married. Since Dad got married so soon, he wanted us children to be with him. And of course Mom wanted us too. Being wanted by both parents is something else when you as a child need to decide which parent you want. We both stayed with our mother. The trauma of the divorce was enough without a move and without learning to know a new mother.

In the game of divorce, children are the pawns. The price we children have to pay for our parents' divorces is astronomical. It cannot be measured. An entire lifetime can never pay the price. The agony of choosing, or of not choosing because of not being able, kills the heart and life of a child. The struggle to make that kind of a choice is unnatural. It should never be demanded of a child. That's why I gave my baby away to be adopted. It killed me all over again, of course. But I couldn't stand to see my baby go through what I went through as a child.

A child is psychologically cut in two when his love for the two people who care for him as mother and father must be severed. A child's greatest right is love and to know love through enduring human relationships. Whether parents are natural parents, foster parents, or adoptive parents, the child needs love from them to learn how to love. The first two years of a child's life are when the love bonds between parents and child are formed. If these bonds aren't formed, the child's ability to establish enduring relationships in later life is disrupted.

I couldn't bear to give my child less than the best. I would have been less than the best. I wanted to be sure my child got proper love at the outset of life. Even before six months of age a baby clearly distinguishes between the faces and voices of parents and those of strangers. I wanted to be sure my baby had a permanent home so that those distinctions are not constantly being fuzzed. Between six and twelve months love is already so binding that separation even for a day or two will bring distress with refusal to eat, restless sleep, and other signs of grief. The cost to the child cannot be estimated. It may affect the child for years to come.

Children sense a violation of trust at an extremely early age. They aren't sure they can extend their love then to you. Their real attachment to someone cannot really happen as it should. I could not sentence my child to emotional destruction. The chance to love and be loved comes only once and it should come at the proper time. I had been emotionally destroyed. I can live with it. But I didn't want my child to have to know that part of life.

Soon after my father was gone, I wanted a father. I kept asking my mother for a father. She seemed to get back on her feet spiritually and emotionally. She was so good to us. She felt bad that she couldn't get me a father. So I began to pray for a father!

We were always taught to pray about everything when we were little. Mother didn't object to my praying for another father. But it seemed the more I prayed the longer it took for an answer to come. I felt wounded at church when I'd mention my father and the others would snicker at me.

At school I was called a PK. That means preacher's kid. I felt isolated. They would dictate to me what I was to do and what I was not to do because I was a PK. I didn't have all that many friends, to tell you the truth. I really needed someone like my father. I missed him so much. I ached—physically ached—from wanting him so much.

Well, I was ready to give up. But my faith was rewarded. After what seemed many, many years, a man came into my mother's life. When they finally announced their plans to be married, Mom had to leave the church and give up her membership. Can you think of anything more heathenish? Or pagan?

Anyhow, that man came into our lives, not only Mom's. What a swell man. He was salve to our wounds. Healing began to take place. We were not well overnight. Nor were the scars removed. But Mom began to care all over again in a much deeper way, like she used to. This man cared deeply for us, too. To this day, I thank God for answering one of the most important prayers in my life.

My brother and I broke our parents' hearts when both of our marriages ended in divorce. You see, this man my mother married as her second husband was also a divorcee. His situation was like Mom's, only switched. They had hoped that their being together would make up to us some of the bruises we had known and suffered earlier. They felt wretched and grieved when they realized our lives had been permanently damaged and their efforts to salvage us before it was too late seemed futile. When my brother and I got divorced our parents seemed to go through their individual divorce grief all over again. I felt so badly for them—and yet helpless, caught in the situation I was.

My brother began running around with a bad crowd of guys a bit older than himself. He was probably looking for some type of father-image that he missed during the years our mother was without a husband and we were without a father. Anyhow, he got into trouble with the law. The other guys almost always pinned the blame on him. Mother was called out many nights to go to jail and get her son. He resented almost every effort to help him. Rather than coming home and talking things over with me, he stayed away.

He began living with a girl. A pregnancy resulted. He came to his senses enough to feel he should marry the girl. But their wedding had no basis of commitment. There was nothing they could attach their marriage to and nothing they could attach themselves to. They were so young. I hurt so deeply inside for him that I can't really talk about his misfortunes.

Now, in my own case, my first father was so likable and my second father was so tender, I assumed that all men were like my two fathers at face value. So I blindly married a fellow who wasn't all I might have hoped for underneath the surface. But I believed we would have had a marvelous marriage after some years of working at it and lots of time spent with its development.

At the outset of our marriage he couldn't keep a job. He was always buying another car, always wanting this or that. Finally he realized those things were not the answers to his restlessness. He told me he was going to settle down and that I was to quit my job and have a baby. He did and I did. But one night he went out with an old gang of his to celebrate our baby's arrival. And someone mixed the wrong kind and amounts of dope and alcohol. He blew his mind. He has an irreversibly damaged brain.

I was legally advised to proceed with a divorce so that he could be kept the rest of his life in an institution and I would not be liable for the expenses. I went back into nursing full time again. I asked my church if I could maybe serve as primary department superintendent. I wanted to know about all the children in our church and not just one class. I felt I had a gift of understanding for any child who might be going through family turmoil. I felt qualified to be of some value there and hoped they would use me.

"But, our church has a policy" they said. "We are sorry that we cannot use you, but. . . ." You know how it goes. That same old holier than thou line. I felt my divorce was legitimate—unless the church wanted to pick up the expense account for my husband's tragedy. I know God's feelings about divorce. He said in Malachi that He hates divorce. I know that. But God is a Father—my Father. He wants what's best for me. I don't think He's a legalist.

I went for counseling. I felt confused. I would have gone back to my parents, but I knew their hearts were already bleeding for me. I felt I needed to get some answers. Then I could go back to them and share what I learned.

My counselor happened to be a person who came to the church group I joined later. Since I'm a nurse, he put my problem in medical terms so that I could grasp the concept. He emphasized the compassionate side of God, my Father, and likened Him to a doctor who has a patient who is diabetic. The diabetes may have become so severe that healing cannot take place in the diabetic body, especially in the feet. If healing cannot take place and gangrene has a chance to set in, or if circulation in the leg stops and the foot turns black, the last thing the surgeon wants to do, but *must* do, is to remove the foot or leg.

He said the same principle can be applied to my case. The last thing I might have wanted to happen was what happened. Now that it has happened, I must do something to save the life that is there—mine and the baby's. God's compassion far exceeds man's legalism. Though the legalism may have caused me to need to leave the church, God never made me leave His heart. I am still there. And that's comforting. What a wonderful God we have, in spite of the messes we get ourselves into.

My counselor advised me to consider leaving the area, especially since I decided by myself to give up my baby. He felt I could start over better somewhere else. So I came here. I'm glad God led me here. He never abandons His children, they abandon Him.

* * *

Norma next interviewed a nurse who was the victim of the unhappy marriage of her parents. Her childhood was badly scarred by hostile feelings between her father and mother.

This young woman was able to remember details about her early trauma; she readily admitted to her own aversion to marriage, her fear of men, and her pervading aloneness.

In the comments that follow, she mentions an angle on divorce which she terms "childrens' rights." Children, she feels, should have the right to depend on their parents' emotional maturity and stability because children are the true victims of unhappy marriages.

It seems to me it was a tragedy for my parents not to get a divorce. It was their main topic of discussion while I grew up. I felt after a while that they talked about divorce openly just to upset me. Unless they were so upset themselves about it and with each other that they weren't aware of my perception.

There are specific things a child should not have to hear his parents say—a couple dozen things, I suppose. One parent will tell a child to tell the other parent something. One parent will use a child to spy on the other parent. Parents will make a child the buffer between them. One parent will tell the child faults of the other parent. One parent will use the child to supply needs that should be supplied by the other parent. Loneliness is an example there.

One parent will down the other parent in front of the child. One parent will list his own good points to the other parent in front of the child. One parent will say specific things to the child about the other parent, like, "Your father makes me so angry." Or, "Your father is a bum." Or, "Your mother can't hold a job. I'll buy your bike for you."

This kind of feuding demoralizes a child. He vacillates back and forth between loyalties to each parent. And he never knows security and stability. Parents should be the stable and constant element in a child's world. Feuding makes that world come apart. And when a parent is one of the persons who makes that world come apart, then angry, hostile, and ambivalent feelings are the inevitable result. Look at me. I'm a classic example.

A child ought to be given certain rights at birth. These rights need to be established by the parents. Respect for the child—that's a right. The right for the child's neutrality, never to be brought into an argument by either parent. If a child wants to know what an argument is about to assure himself that he is not in it or that it is not over *him*, he has a right to know that. He also has the right not to take sides—the thing he least wants to do, but is often trapped into doing. He has the right to be loved dearly by both parents and not used by either. He has a right to be safe with each of his parents.

That right should be stamped on the baby's birth certificate. It should be framed above the child's bed for the parents to read daily. This business of getting married and then having free license to continue on an immature marriage-go-round ought to be outlawed.

My parents psychologically manipulated each other treacherously. But they had the gall to stay married to each other. One would do something nice for the other and then use that deed as a handle to manipulate the other to get something he or she wanted. Like "I fixed your favorite pancakes this morning. Now you fix the faucet tonight." That doesn't give the other person a chance to do anything out of love. They do it as if being led by the nose. That gets old quick!

Another example is to make the other feel guilty if she didn't fix those pancakes. Like "I fixed the faucet. When will I get my pancakes?" It makes one want to throw a whole plate of pancakes in his face! And the syrup down over his head! Life is hard enough without having agitating episodes constantly happening like that.

My parents' main problem was immaturity—emotional immaturity. I know that divorce is conceding to a failure to adjust to an important adult relationship. I know there is a better chance of happiness by staying together and sticking it out and working at it than by going it alone or with another partner. But this is true only if the partners are mature. I can see the problem of in-laws, money, and infidelity causing divorce. But when you get into emotional problems, you have something that's far more damaging than divorce. Everybody ought to be able to work out almost any kind of problem. But the emotionally immature personality is not equipped to do so. It's like a flaw in a piece of material; it will not hold up under pressure or tension. It ruptures. This type of person cannot process a marriage to maturity.

I understand that a good, growing relationship needs periodic evaluation. You evaluate yourself and you evaluate each other. This is done to make the glue stick or the seam stay stitched. To think that there are problem marriages and that they can be dissolved is a myth. There are no problem marriages. There are only problem people. Marriage is a maturing process. It becomes a problem process when the people in it are problems. Couples must work together at making marriage a maturing process. When that cannot or does not happen, I say throw it out the window.

When I was little, I remember seeing my mom sit on the side of the bed and cry. She would go upstairs to cry, she never cried in front of Dad. I'd follow her up there and sit beside her. I was always puzzled at why she was crying.

Even though I had four older brothers, I had a

bed to myself and a room to myself. Many nights I would hear the screen door open on the porch below my room. I'd get up, go to my window, and distressingly watch Dad quietly get into the car, back out of the drive, and keep the car lights off. I'd sit there as long as I could and watch for him to come back. I guess I'd fall asleep or finally go back to bed. I don't ever remember being at the window when he drove in.

The next day he'd show up. But never for breakfast. My heart grew sadder each time he drove away those nights. It was really traumatic to me. I never talked about it. Nor did I ask any of my brothers if they ever heard Dad drive out.

I was so burdened about my parents not being able to get along that, when I was a teenager, I said something to one of my friends. Our church had a summer picnic. My friend and I were in a boat alone. As I was rowing I burst out, "Oh, Sharon, I don't know what to do!"

"What's the matter?" she asked me. She was concerned. She'd never seen me that agitated.

"My folks just don't get along at all. And I cannot stand it any longer! What am I going to do?" I pleaded. I really shocked her. Her mouth dropped open. She stared at me in disbelief.

Then she said, "That's impossible! Why, Becky, your folks are pillars of our church. If ever there was an ideal couple, it's your mom and dad. I can't believe what you're saying."

"Maybe it's just me," I said and kept rowing. I never talked to her again about my parents. Nor to any of my other friends for that matter.

And then to make a liar out of me, Mom got

pregnant! She was forty-eight. Just what we needed, wasn't it? A baby, years behind us all. And that had a taint of tragedy in it too. Jimmy was born severely retarded.

That was quite a shock to all of us, including the church people. No one seemed to know how to relate to us. Responses varied from avoiding us like we were the plague or lepers to "we know God has a purpose in all things" recitations. As I look back now, I'm sure it was an ego blow to both my parents. Especially my dad. Just as they fought passionately, they also loved passionately. And this retarded baby might have made them question the ability of their only means of staying together. And of course, they knew they needed to stay together now to keep this baby and care for him. And Jimmy did seem to join their hearts a bit closer than before.

I took my college degree in special education, mainly because of my brother's mental handicap. I won a scholarship for school and I couldn't pass it up. It was an invaluable two years of study after nurses' training. At first I didn't want to work in special ed. I wanted to stay in nursing. But the combination of special ed and nursing go hand in hand very well. The visual, hearing, and speech handicapped children which I have worked with in nursing are a part of special education. We had cerebral palsied children in the hospital. They are special ed concerns—as well as the entire area of retardation from mongoloidism to the vocationally rehabilitated employee.

I panicked over dating. I finally gave up getting married. I decided I wouldn't make the kind of wife I had dreamed a wife was to be. I was afraid I couldn't accept guilt or work it through. I was afraid I couldn't cope like I might wish. I didn't want a repeat of my parents' life. So I decided at twenty-five that I preferred to be single. I weighed certain things in the scales, like my profession, my independence, my self-development, my ability to make money and travel and decided it could compensate for marriage.

I've had to take time to understand myself. Often I don't like what I see. I try to improve myself if I can. I've had to realize that everyone has problems, whether married or single. So I try to be objective about life. I realize rebellion intensifies problems. So I stay away from that monster. I've wanted to become a credit to being single. That means I've needed to develop positive attitudes about myself, like telling myself I'm a person of worth. I accept my being single by remembering I'm a woman whether I'm single or married. I try to be self-giving. I realize that someday I will be responsible in some way for Jimmy. I want to be self-giving then too. So I'm working on self-development.

The Census Bureau says that the number of people living alone jumped three million from 1969 to 1974. More than 30 million single women now live in the United States.

So, what does a single woman do? Good question. My first response would be that the biological needs and drives wage a battle in all people, which calls for strong inner resources to resist and not abuse.

The moral casualties we see today may mean that help from outside of ourselves is required. I had to have some. I learned that some women say the fight is not worth the effort. They claim the buildup of sexual tensions cannot be avoided. And in some "form" or another they yield to deviant behavior and say they can't help it. I had problems here. That's why I gave up at twenty-five and said I'd remain single. Then when I got to working with my defeated, guilty feelings, I worked my way out of that conflict. It's amazing how swiftly personality deterioration sets in.

I also learned that some women maintain a form of morality, but are having immoral fantasies. This may be a carry-over from normal childhood daydreaming, but it's hardly a healthy approach to adult sexuality. Also I learned that some women become angry with God as well as themselves and try to blame God that their needs and drives have to be restrained.

But I say use your head! Think about the starving refugees in Asia. Think about the hungry-for-a-sugar cookie diabetic. Then discipline yourself to avoid sexually stimulating situations or activities which build frustration. Don't watch stimulating movies; don't read sexy books. Then if you still can't control yourself, commit your total being, including your sex drives and desires, to a Being greater than yourself, to the God who created you. Remember that those drives and desires are not wrong in themselves. It's the un-natural, deviant yielding to them that is wrong. We may all be tempted at some point, but we don't have to yield.

The Apostle Paul talked about this same struggle in 1 Corinthians 7:7 and 32-35. He proclaimed victory in Christ Jesus. For me, devotion to Christ is the best antidote for temptation. Christ surely isn't going to erase my needs and desires, or my sexual drives. He didn't take away my need for water, food, or oxygen when I became devoted to Him. Basic drives and desires remain the same, I'm convinced, but I make a distinction by saying that Christ meets the deepest needs and desires of the soul. Sex is not necessary for inner peace and spiritual fulfillment.

I have contentment in Christ, purpose in life, meaning, freedom, acceptance, and assurance, to name a few things. Those things are certainly different than lack of security in love and deep bodily hungers, sexual or otherwise. But, not to be hung up on those things is to get them into their proper place.

When Christ is given His proper place within us, those other things become subordinate.

*   *   *

The stories could go on and on. There's little question that divorce is a tragedy in life equal to a serious accident or a debilitating illness. Behind the words of the subjects who were willing to tell their stories lies obvious pain, confusion, and spiritual struggle.

As Norma went on with her interviews the matter of sex became a more and more noticeable factor in these casualty cases. More often than not sex problems were the major factor in the divorce—whether through actual sexual troubles in the marriage itself, temptations outside of the marriage, or downright adultery in the life of one or both of the partners.

Adultery is sin, all Christians agree. But as the Savior frankly observed, "The flesh is weak."

Norma found, in her continued interviewing, that divorced Christians were most realistic about sex, and willing to talk about it. They had all been there and back where this troublesome part of life is concerned.

Norma groups their experiences under the heading, "The Sex Hex."

3

The Sex Hex

Betty Ford said Sunday, "I wouldn't be surprised" if her daughter Susan, 18, decided to have an affair. The First Lady suggested that in general premarital relations with the right partner might lower the divorce rate. . . . Commenting further on her attitude toward premarital love affairs, she said there seems to be "a complete freedom among the young people now. . . ."—United Press International, Washington, August 11, 1975, report on the appearance of Mrs. Gerald Ford on the TV show, *Sixty Minutes*.

Thou shalt not commit adultery. —Exodus 20:14

It seems, in view of the foregoing quotations, that the powers on earth and the Power in heaven sharply disagree about sex. There was some disagreement in certain sectors of the church as well:

I'm happy to see her at least mention such things and talk about them. They too often get ignored and hushed up."—Marion Malonson, president, Washington state chapter of Church Women United, reported by Associated Press, August 12, 1975.

That's gutter type mentality . . . that's animal
thinking . . . to say that in general premarital relations might lower the divorce rate is evil and hate-
ful.—Dr. W. A. Criswell, pastor, First Baptist
Church, Dallas, Texas, August 12, 1975 (quoted in
Dallas Morning News, p. 2).

The *Dallas Morning News*, which ran all of the
above quotes (except the unpopular selection
from the Book of Exodus) offered an editorial
later in the week after the dust had settled a bit.
The *News* felt that Mrs. Ford was to blame:

First, for not having [Interviewer] Safer thrown
out on his ear, second, for answering in such terms
as contravene historic Judeo-Christian morality.

The euphemism, "historic Judeo-Christian
morality," serves in place of the unjournalistic
"God" or "The Bible," which might have been
more appropriate, or at least more emphatic. But
the editorial writer clearly felt the president's
wife was out of line:

For the wife of the president to theorize that premarital sex might cut the divorce rate—well, just
say that it was unbecoming and uncalled for. . . . In
any case, Mrs. Ford ought to remember herself—
she is the First Lady of the land. If she seriously
believes the moral law has no more meaning, she
would be wise to keep her beliefs to herself.

Mrs. Ford also addressed the issues of women
in government and drug-taking with the same
bone-crushing tact, but let's consider one sin at a
time. The subject at hand is sex, specifically sex

as related to marriage and divorce. Sex places a hex on marriages and people in general, one by one, and is seemingly an important feature of every divorce case. Christians perform sex and unbelievers perform sex. Even animals and plants perform their versions of this God-created exercise for continuing life on earth. Sex is a dynamic, problematic, vitally important facet of success or failure in life, modern thinkers of every persuasion agree.

Researcher Martin might have written volumes of her own opinion on the ramifications of sex in marriage and divorce, but in keeping with the spirit of her research project she instead went out among the people again. The exact words of the casualties, and the feelings apparent behind them, tell in a different way than the theories of the experts, what is involved in this emotionally charged area. We will, of course, consult the theories of the experts, but it has never been very clear whether there really are any "experts" on sex.

Now of course asking about sex is different than asking, "What happened the night your spouse departed?" Many divorced people were willing to give their testimonies about their divorces in great detail, or maybe they were eager to present their side of the story. But only a few wanted to hash out their own sex problems, or the sexual difficulties in their marriages. Probably there is no other topic so often talked about, from the First Lady of the land on down, than the problem of sex, but as Mark Twain lamented in connection with the weather, "Nobody ever does anything about it."

Coauthor Martin had to be quite tactful in securing interviews about sex among her Christian friends. Because of the taboos, stigmas, and sensitivities of those she interviewed, she had to take special care with her own questions and comments to elicit useful information germane to a subject like this one.

It should also be said, in connection with the following interviews, that Norma was dealing with Christians. The sex problems and divorces of Christians are in some sort of class by themselves, a researcher quickly discovers. Sex problems and even divorce are sometimes considered sophisticated among the unbelievers, as if they are up with modern times and thus participate in the current cultural hang-ups. Advocates of the New Morality, whatever that is, bear their disabilities from the new morality in the manner that the great German fencing champions bore their fencing scars. There's almost a sense of pride today, among the free-thinking new generation, in having a life filled with emotional trauma and in visiting "my analyst." So Betty Ford was able to take a stab at being "with it" in her rather disconcerting pronouncements about the new American condition.

Christians, on the other hand, widely regard sexual problems, and especially divorce, as sure signs of spiritual failure. Many suffer as much from the severity of the local church as from the problems themselves.

Thus, in getting these particular interviews, the researcher was embarking on an area fraught with a double hazard—sex and the special stigma of spiritual defeat. She had to be most careful.

Norma kept a virtual diary on this part of her research, leaving the tape recorder running and commenting into it between interviews. There are offhand conversations about marriage in general, small-talk, and all of the normal interrelating of human beings in the following section. The dialogue material, where Norma was able to talk at length with two divorced Christians— Mary Jane and Gail—is one-of-a-kind.

Here's Norma's complete record of Sex Hex:

Since I had the upcoming night off and could sleep, I decided to stay up and get ready for my club luncheon early and do some shopping on my way to the luncheon. I remembered something I had read which said that the most frequent source of conflict in life is in the whole field of sexuality. Our confidence is determined there as well as our personality and individuality. Understanding our sexuality is a great fortress against crises that we cannot cope with. A healthy attitude toward oneself usually develops into a happy life and a feeling toward others that grows into good love relationships.

The luncheon was as usual food-wise, but unusual social-wise. Somehow we got started on my subject by Mary saying she has learned how to "treat" Stan, her husband, to get best results. "I say, 'Thank you, Stan, for doing that for me,' or for the way he points up my faults to me. I make sure I tell him I appreciate it. 'You are making me a better person, Stan, by pointing that out to me, and consequently you will have a better wife for it,' I say. And don't you know, he responds better to me. He is kinder, more thoughtful to me. And then he usually gets what he wants. And I think it makes us both better sex partners," she explained.

"Well, now, that's not the way I read it this morning," I said teasingly. "I read that it's the vow and not sex that carries you through."

"Don't you tell Bill that!" said Susan. "He'd call that hogwash!" she continued.

"You'd better believe it," added Erma. "Things are going good for LeRoy and me. Let's not put any stumbling blocks in our way. Let good enough alone." she admonished. "I could not be happier with the relationship LeRoy and I have now."

"What did you do?" asked Ferne. "I need to know. I could use some help."

"The hex of sex comes when either of you make demands on the other," offered Lois. "You're in for trouble then for sure. Ask me, I know," she said.

"Well, for me the hex of sex is something different," stated Lucille. "Because I'm older than any of you, I might look at sex differently. But I'm going through Gilder's book, *Sexual Suicide*. He says that when men and women deny their divergent sexuality, they reject the deepest sources of love and identity. They commit sexual suicide because they become shapeless, dissolute things in destructive pursuit of ever more elusive pleasures by ever more drastic techniques. So keep your specific identity and your deepest sources of love. That's why your husband chose you in the first place, probably. He saw a specific identity and his identity was attracted to it. He wants *you*," she said.

"I like that," I said. And we continued talking about related subjects until I had to excuse myself to go to Mary Jane's house.

Mary Jane was a bit low. She said car sales are down where she works, and she's afraid she'll be permanently laid off. "You wouldn't believe how much the profits have dropped. Our officers in the company and the managers aren't getting any bonuses like they did last year. The drop in sales is depressing, and I don't even own the company. Think how the owner feels," she mused out loud.

"Have you been doing something for yourself to help lift your spirits?" I asked.

"I'm reading *The Love-Fight* by David Augsburger. He makes me feel better, like I haven't lost all of life's battles. But sometimes it seems I'm a loser," she said.

"What's been happening in your life the last while?" I queried.

"I moved to a bigger apartment the other week. I have three bedrooms now. The kids sure like it better too. They like the extra space we have. And then I broke up with a guy I was going with. I was so involved with him. I was more involved than I wanted to be. I couldn't put up with his demands and approaches. Then to top it off, I found out that he's married. So I had to stop seeing him."

"Does he give up easily?" I asked.

"No," she answered. "Something is in my car every Sunday morning when I go out to go to church. He was spending his week ends here with me. He called three to four times a week, after he had been here every night of the week. So something in the car once a week isn't much compared to how things were. I'm not proud of my life with him. In fact, I'm quite disgusted with myself, though not really ashamed," she said.

"Are the sex aspects of your life a bugaboo to you?" I tried to ask nonchalantly.

"Oh, maybe. I'd kind of like to find another guy. But I can accept it if one doesn't show up, now that I just got rid of this one. Even though I don't go out a lot, I need a guy for social functions," she stated.

"How about needing a guy for sexual functions?" I asked.

"Well, if I don't think about it, I'm not climbing the wall. I guess I haven't really worked that out. I'm trying to ignore it, since I haven't been able to work through it. You see, I went 1 1/2 years without sex after my divorce from my first husband. I went through hell because of it. I was up nights. I took cold showers. And I was having inner battles. I finally felt the battles we had been through were easier in retrospect than what I was going through. So I remarried the guy. I'm glad I did, but he died three years later of cancer. He was in his middle twenties. When he was so sick and dying and we could not have sex, I changed some of my views about sex."

60

"How do you mean?" I asked.

"I didn't think I could give up sex. But now that I realize a bit better what love and commitment is, I feel that they belong with sex somehow. When you find a person you love (and because he was so ill and needed me as a person), you see the unimportance of sex and the importance of a person. You can give up your own needs for the sake of that person's needs. You find fulfillment that way.

"Once I thought that unless you are married, you should forget sex. But my thinking is changed on that. Sex is here. It is good. God gave it to us, so use it, I thought. Then I changed to sex is okay if no one gets hurt. Now I believe that you cannot have good sex if a commitment is lacking. However, I must hasten to say that I don't want to give up sex because I enjoy it so very much. If I can find a man I love, sex will be worth waiting for. If I can't, I may not be able to wait."

"So, what do you do in the meantime?" I asked.

"I get very restless, very cranky. I take life out on me when things go bad at the office or here at home with my five kids. I feel sorry for poor me. I think no one loves me. I feel rotten when I don't have any physical attention. I need closeness. I enjoy sex because of the closeness I need and feel. When my old boyfriend comes around and holds me in his arms and calls me a sexy lady, I feel warmer but not necessarily sexy. I need close warm relationships. And I'm trying to find it in other areas than just having a man in my life.

"I'm not sure I'm ready to commit myself to another man right away again. The divorces, separations, and remarriages I've had in the past ten years of my life have called for changes and more changes. I'm not sure I can keep up. I'm trying to accept change. I'm trying to get good feelings about myself. Although I have trouble making decisions yet, I want to be totally in control of my life sooner or later," she said.

"It's really a struggle for you, isn't it?" I tried to say encouragingly.

"Yes. Each divorce and each remarriage brought change. I wasn't able to keep up. I developed colitis. I got periodic headaches. I passed out. I couldn't work. I couldn't take care of my kids. I couldn't take care of myself. I felt totally useless and out of control. And I wanted to be in control. I'm trying to get in touch with me. The changes are becoming more and more scary. You don't get colitis one day and get rid of it the next day. These problems plague me. I guess I need my problems though. Do you know what I do when I feel useless, how I pick my spirits up?" she asked.

"No, and I'm almost afraid to guess," I answered with a smile.

"I feel good if I can make a man feel good. My main function in life until now has been to please a man. I feel good if I can make a man feel a hero. Since my one problem is that I want a man, it so happens that I pick guys that are no good," she answered.

"What do you mean when you say 'no good'?" I asked.

"I choose a loser. I can be comfortable with a loser. I expect to be hurt. This proves to me that guys are no good. And losers are easier to attract than winners. I've been a loser in the past myself. Therefore I pick those of like nature. One feels comfort with people who are like you. But now I'm changing. It's beautiful. I'm trying to get in touch with myself. It's hard to see oneself grow. That makes the struggle greater sometimes. And it doesn't put me beyond the temptation of wanting to go to bed with a guy when one comes around."

"Do many come around?" I asked.

"Oh, yeah. I get phone calls from guys every week. Three different guys call each week. One guy calls me four times a week. It's fascinating. With one of the guys, I feel very comfortable and I don't expect anything to grow out of it. Another of the other guys is ready to make a commitment to me. If things work out, he would like to have me be his wife. But he does not open up and share with me like I wish he would.

"And before I get married again, there would need to be a senior partner in our marriage—God. I've had all these disasters in my life so far because I didn't know God nor was I committed to Him and yielded to Him. It must be different now.

"The other guy and I agree on everything. We even agree that we could not get along. We both are being turned on to Christ though. But we know we cannot make each other happy. He is judgmental and I cannot live with that. After we've decided we are not going to be married, we have each other as friends. He's my sounding board now," she said.

"Does that exclude sex?" I dared to ask.

"That's weird. Sometimes it does. Sometimes it doesn't. If I'm not needing sex, I don't bring it up. We've been friends long enough that we have sex. We've been having sex. And then there's my ex-husband, one of them. He comes around about once a month. But he never asks sex of me. It happens sometimes though, even though he never asks for it. Our relationship is beyond comprehension. I tolerate it and at the same time like it. I like it, mainly to see that I made the right decision to leave him. All his ideas differ totally from mine."

"Do you think you could pick out a winner for a husband?" I asked.

"Well, my pattern is to love losers. I feel compassion for them. I can flatter a person. I'm learning to turn that inward, though, so maybe I could. I used to focus my view on my losing. Now I am absorbing, digesting things. I'm at an input stage. I'm reading books like *Born to Win, & Born to Lose.* I'm living more on thinking and less on feeling. My life-pattern has been to go by feeling. And that went in spurts. I hope to level off, balance out.

"One day I'll tell myself that I need a man in my life for input, for warmth and not for sex. I say that I've been fighting to get single: I don't want to get involved with anyone. And then I feel the pull go to the other extreme and I wonder how I can exist without a man in my life. I stop to think about it a minute and I realize that there has always been a man, or men, in my life.

"Then I tell myself that I have colitis and am dying for some highly seasoned pizza. I know I can't have any. I tell myself that if I'm patient, one of these days I may dare have pizza once again when I get my colitis under control. In the same way, I'm dying for sex. I don't have to give it up: I have to wait. Not having to give it up, but waiting for it makes it possible for me to live with the thought. Knowing me, I may not be able to wait if I don't find a man I can love, which would make sex worth waiting for," she stated.

"Vicious cycle, isn't it?" I said.

"Yes, and I keep telling myself that flour alone doesn't make a cake. It's an essential ingredient; you wouldn't have a cake without it. So sex is an important part of life. But sex alone without a commitment, without other ingredients will not make a life," she answered.

"I keep telling myself that I have been a failure as a married person. But I know that's not what God wants me to focus on. I believe in the forgiveness aspect of life. I believe every individual is a person of value, at least in God's eyes. Divorce may carry a stigma for us people down here on earth. But we all do have value. We have had it all along. I think Christ can lead us to it. He is showing it to me. That's why I'm reading my Bible a lot. I believe that I can get straightened out yet in life. I really believe it." she said emphatically and with a degree of determination to prove that to herself.

"Sounds good. Keep it up and keep at it. You can make it with your determination channeled in the direction you're headed," I encouraged. "I see that I have to be on my way. Time goes too fast, doesn't it? Your children will soon be home from school. You should have a few minutes to yourself before they come. So I'll be going. I'll be in touch with you again, probably Sunday. Right?"

"I suppose. My days get pretty full and hectic during the week," she replied.

"Do have a good week," I said as I left.

On my way home I thought about an earlier conversation with Kate. I listened to the tape I had made of our discussion:

"My biggest conflict is on the sex issue," she said. "Some of my friends tell me to take care of myself. If I need sex, okay. See that I get it. Now that's not the way I've been taught. That's not the way I believe and that's not what I think my Bible says. You know the whole business. So this is something I have to work through."

"Let's be sure we're on the same wave length," I said. "Tell me what you're thinking about when you say 'sex.'"

"I guess 'sex' can cover a vast area. It's not only the act. I like somebody to be with. I like somebody that appreciates the way I look and thinks that what I do is great and this sort of thing. But at my age you can't go with somebody for an awfully long time and keep it at that phase.

"I have to decide what it is that I want now. Do I want companionship? An occasional date? Sex? Somebody to be with me, to like me and the way I look? Is it somebody's arms around me that I want? Exactly what is it I want? Is it just a father for my children? I don't want a father for my children. They're quite capable of taking care of themselves," she continued in deep thought as I listened.

"Uh-huh."

"On the other hand, I was going with a guy who was a very good listener and he thought I could do no wrong. My doctor was telling me he thought that must be great. And I said, 'After all I've been through, I guess it should be, but it isn't balanced.' "

"Did you think this guy you were going with was buttering you up?" I inquired.

"Well, I think he honestly thought I'd never get angry at him and, you know, I'm not all that bad of a person when I'm in my right mind. When I get out on a date, I act nice, just like everyone else does. I realized this guy hadn't lived with me nor had I ever been angry at him. And me being angry at somebody is something else!"

"He never saw you upset then?"

"He saw when I was upset at my children. He didn't like the way they treated me. That upset him very much. He felt they should have more respect for me than they did."

"Did you feel he wanted to come in and protect you then somehow?"

"He didn't. Sometimes he would help to do some of the painting here in the house. Sometimes when I was working with the children and I'd be talking with them, he said he felt that I showed more patience than his wife had who left him with three kids. He said, 'If I'd have had to put up with what you did, I'd have never made it. My kids weren't fighting me all the time like yours are.' So I think I had more than one problem. It's not only the divorce. It's the way I work with my children. I thought I was working with them so that they would be free to talk and free to say what they wanted to say so that I could at least cope with that aspect of my life. But I can't seem to take their anger when it's directed at me."

"What's your standing with this fellow you were dating?" I asked.

"We broke up. Going with him, having him here, and dating him made me realize I was still in love with Stanley. But for what, I don't know! Being in contact with this guy and feeling the closeness of another man made me aware I was still holding on to Stanley. I couldn't give in to this guy sexually and then I understood why. I came around quicker in my thinking on sex and marriage by having gone with this guy. When I realized what I felt about Stanley, I knew there was no use seeing this guy anymore. So I broke up with him."

"Well, what was the main problem between you and Stanley?"

"I felt that he wanted me to act like his mother whom he hates. I was to play the stern mother role for him, but act like his wife as far as sex was concerned. There was that love-hate thing going on between us all the time. He would accept my love which didn't always include sex. My love

68

wasn't always sex. Often it was baking his favorite cookies, that kind of thing. That was my way of showing him when I was sorry sometimes. I don't know, I don't know. It's a big mixed-up mess, I'll tell you that," she answered.

"Having loved him as an expression of 'I'm sorry. Will you forgive me?' rather than loving him as an expression of adoration, devotion, and 'I love you for you' you cheated both you and him, didn't you?" I asked.

"You have me stumped there. I think I see the difference although it is a bit hazy in my mind."

"Perhaps he wasn't wanting a token offering of love or gesture of cookies. Maybe he wanted you, just you," I tried to explain. "Just the beautiful giving of yourself, your total being. Am I being too hard on you by saying that?"

"What did affect me, I believe, is that I felt that he was getting what he needed and I was not getting what I needed. He didn't care much about that though. What I felt I really needed was companionship. He had none of that to give, it seemed. So for a long time, when he wanted sex I would say, 'Well if you want sex just go ahead. I can't.' And that's because I was so angry inside that I knew right from the beginning—from the time I was married to him—that if he didn't have sex, I would lose him. I guess that's probably why we were together as long as we were."

"Because you gave him what he wanted?" I reflected.

"Um-huh, and when I couldn't I would let him go on and he got his satisfaction. I didn't. I was mad at him. My counselor said, 'Well, he did exactly what you said but you're mad at him for it.' That's true, but I guess I was hoping. He knew how I responded when I was being fulfilled. He knew that. And he left a year go by and it didn't bother him at all. I wanted help. I realized I needed help. I asked for it and he didn't. He thought it was all in my head. And it was. I'm probably not as affectionate as some people. But I think the reason I couldn't respond to him was because of my hostility for him. It was in my head."

"It was a mental barrier which would not allow your body to function and perform?" I questioned.

"Uh-huh."

"But he wouldn't get angry for you not responding to him or with him?"

"No, he wouldn't."

"As long as he was satisfied, he was okay. And you were wanting companionship," I commented.

"Well, he didn't like it. But after a while I think he just kind of took it for granted, thinking 'Well, if that's the way she wants to be, okay.' He didn't like it, that's true. He would much have preferred to have me try. But after a while, toward the end, I just said, 'I absolutely can't.' After that is when I believe he started probably thinking about elsewhere and that type of thing. I guess my idea for saying, 'I absolutely can't,' which was absolutely true, was that I was hoping we could get help. But it took the opposite turn. Instead, he left for someone else rather than work through it. That was it. That's what really made me cry."

"Did you cry?" I asked.

"Yeah. He was saying I wasn't worth helping. Someone else could take my place. I was a cast-off. I felt that I had done a lot of things to help our marriage work. I thought I had taken a lot more than married women would have. I'm not one to run. And rather than facing the problem and working it through he went the other direction. And here I am."

"Do you think he needed an easy way out?"

"Uh-huh. He'd have also had to look inside himself. I told him once that someday there's going to be a place that he can't run from. Someday there's going to be a place where he can't hide. I don't know when that day is going to be or where but someday he's going to get there."

"Did he like to hear that? Did he do things that upset you after that?"

"He did. And one time when we were in an office taking a test, one of the graphs revealed something that surprised me. It surprised him too. His self-image was lower than mine on the whole thing. And I felt at that time I was really feeling low in my self-image. But he doesn't portray a low self-image. What he is inside and what he is outside are miles apart. Very few know what he is really like inside. So I would guess that he has self-hate. He hated me when he left. But he swept other people off their feet. He looked very good. That's why he remarried again right away, I would guess. He has a way of making you like him at first sight."

"What would happen then to his self-image if this marriage he's in now would sort of become a duplication of the one he walked out on?" I asked. "When you think about something like that, do you feel like you wish he would come back? Or don't you have these feelings?"

"I don't know that I can accept him the way he is now," she answered.

"Only with help or therapy?" I questioned.

"I wouldn't go back without therapy. That's absolute. I've had quite a bit and I absolutely would not, for all the hurting and all the anger that I've had toward him, accept him. I don't know if I *could* accept him, you know."

The next morning I hurried off to my 9:00 Bible class where we were studying the Book of Mark. After class Gail and I had arranged to go out to lunch together. She was such a lovely person and I wondered if she had worked through the whole scope of sexuality in her thinking since her divorce. So I asked her.

"Yes, I have," she said. "I had to. You see for years I felt like a machine that one can put a quarter in and get out something that meets needs and desires. A 'sex machine' I guess you'd call it. Well, that's what I felt like. And so I knew I had work to do to transfer my thinking from machine to person and to female in particular. Many times my husband didn't bother to put the quarter in. He just expected me to operate. Pretty soon I felt like a Raggedy Ann sexually. So the divorce—why not? What else would you expect?

"Then those propositions. They were what about threw me off my feet before I could even get on them. I knew I had to search for some kind of meaningful identity. You see, I'm made so different from Romaine. Any guy in pants turned her on. And without pants too! I was confused in my thinking because I felt so abused and used. You know how it is, when you wear one machine out, you trade that one in for a new one. Or you don't bother to trade it in. You discard it or put it in the attic and get a newer more efficient model. I was that machine.

"Well, I was searching for meaningful friendship at least with my female friends. I needed to discover a level of shared thinking and feeling. With my husband, all we shared were a few pounds of flesh. I wanted something more meaningful. I wanted to touch someone on a feeling level, not just a functioning level.

"Knowing I might not find that fast enough without losing some of my own identity in the meantime, I began finding things to read on sexuality. I heard a person speak at a college convocation about sexuality. It began to make sense. I knew I had to rise from the put-a-quarter-in-machine concept of existence to understanding what it meant to be a woman in all my life, to understand myself as a sexual being in everything I do as a female, not just when experiencing sexual desires or expressions.

"I knew I had to realize fulfillment in every area of my life. I needed to find my role as a woman and look for opportunities to serve others in everyday affairs wherever I might be. It dawned on me then that this sexuality I had was and is a gift from God. I must discover and develop it. It dawned on me that my body didn't have to be classified as a machine. It is the handiwork of God. It is good, respectable, useful, and unique. It dawned on me that I am a woman—not a thing, not a possession, not an object for pleasure, not a physical conquest. I am a person, not a dehumanized being, not an exploitation piece, nor a manipulated goody.

"Now I know that as a person I can accept responsibility for what I can do for God and my fellowmen. I can recognize many dimensions in all my relationships with others and seek to fulfill them in loving motivation that will result in the best for others too. I can commit myself to something, to people, to others while remembering my limitations too. I realize I'll not be doing certain things now since I am divorced. But I will accept them as limitations and go on and do what I can for others in the open avenues of my life. And to myself, I will be all that I can be with my self-giving love that has been released in me to bestow upon others as well as myself.

"My past is behind me. I'm forgiven of my mistakes. I'm free from twists that would make me ugly or resentful. I'm free to love more selflessly by loving self-forgetfulness and self-giving. I feel God can guide and control my motives and prompt my decision-making. He made me; He will help me. Rather than just thinking of myself as a sexual being anymore, I can now think of myself as physical, emotional, and spiritual also. It's becoming exciting as I grow and develop into a person, a woman, a female. I nearly memorized David Augsburger's book, *Be All You Can Be*. It made so much sense to me. It gave me something to grab a hold of and to hang onto. His chapters on love and sexuality are excellent, and I needed his chapters on human relations, mistreatment, forgiveness to remold and reshape my life before it was too late. I know now that it's not too late. And I am so grateful," she concluded.

I realized that I had picked at my food the entire time she talked and that my plate was almost empty. She hadn't started on hers. "Let me talk while you eat your lunch. I don't want to see your soup get any colder," I said. I commended her on the many inner resources she called up when she went through her crisis. I affirmed her on how beautifully she was taking a hold of her situation and not becoming ingrown or introverted. Her outlook seemed great too. And she said it was, that she could go on interdependently with others.

As I left Gail that afternoon, I wondered why some divorced people do not seem to make the hurdle while others like Gail breeze along in life and make the best of their altered circumstances and relationships.

What causes the scarring? Who carries the scars? How long do they last? Is the answer that free legal services are now available for divorcees? Is the answer that the traditional grounds for divorce, like adultery, cruelty, desertion, imprisonment, and legal separation are no longer required? Is the answer that divorce in

Arkansas increased 96 percent from 1969 to 1973, for example? Is it that before 1967 few Jews or Catholics were seen in divorce courts, but now that is changing? Around 3 million Roman Catholics are out of the church for divorce-re-marriage reasons. And now mass for these people is given in Boston. Is it because the assembly line of people waiting for divorces includes the poor who cannot pay great alimonies or child support? Is it that the waiting time for getting a divorce has been reduced? Will the new "ritual of divorce" in the book of alternate rituals of the United Methodist church help? Or what is it?

Gail seemed to know a freedom from guilt, anger, self-pity, and the desire to smear her former mate. She didn't let the word "divorce" spell defeat for her. She was busy in a choral group, in doing volunteer work, and in our Bible study. She took advantage of every opportunity that came her way in which she could not participate when she was married. She was active in various organizations. She took her friends out to eat. She changed some of her old habits and patterns and tried to find a new identity.

Gail succeeded mostly because she said she would only take one day at a time, and not worry about long-range goals right away. She filled her loneliness and vacuums with present challenges.

Pain? Yes. Grief? Yes. But Gail refused to let failure, guilt, and shame rule her.

Should Gail and Mary Jane remarry? Should they find new husbands to take the place of the ones they parted from? Isn't there an obvious vacancy in each of these lives?

76

But what will God think if they remarry? What will the local church think? Are they permitted, as Christians, to even consider that alternative? Even if their church families approve of remarriage for one reason or another, will God, who said that He hates divorce, bless the new union? Does God's Word flatly rule for or against remarriage?

Those are involved questions, to say the least. In one instance a Mennonite church spent three years studying them.

We are now going to look at that particular church study which took up the questions of divorce and remarriage historically and in the seventies. The church expended a tremendous effort in terms of research, discussion, and prayerful findings.

The study was inspired, to begin with, by the request of two members who wished to marry but had been divorced in the past. Rather like the case of Randy and Gretchen in chapter 1, the two sought either the wholehearted approval of the church for their planned marriage, or a clear ruling against it which they could understand.

But unlike Randy and Gretchen they found their need for each other imperative. People might take different views of their personal decision, but in any case they found they could not wait three years.

They married and dropped out of the church somewhere along the way.

4

"Let Us Know When You've Decided Our Fate"

The church carried on its definitive examination of the divorce-remarriage question despite the dropout of the couple who had originally inspired the study. Obviously, there would be other cases coming up; apparently the church should have a clearly stated position based on Scripture and adhered to by all members. Since work was already underway, it was continued in the hope that a sound conclusion might be reached in time to rule on future cases.

It wasn't, of course, that the Bible is unclear on divorce and remarriage, or that God's will is utterly unknown. On the contrary, the Scriptures make clear that God hates divorce. Moses allowed it under certain conditions, and Jesus granted the exception, "except it be for fornication [infidelity]." But Jesus went on to say, "Whoever marries a divorced woman commits adultery" (Matthew 5:32).

Doesn't that end it? What's left to discuss? The Scripture seems clear.

Well, some might say (and certainly *have*

said), "All right, remarriage is a sin. Christians are guilty of lots of other sins. Why can't this particular one be as forgiven as the rest? What's the real harm in people marrying who have previously made a mistake? Is it better if they brood without partners the rest of their lives because of a youthful misjudgment?"

The gravity of the problem emerges. God's commands seem clear, but it is often argued that they don't seem to accommodate the present human condition. Divorce is a common response to marital problems these days. Should the church stand fast on the literal interpretation of the Scriptures, or should there be latitude for considering the deep feelings involved in each individual case?

Clearly, there should be no divorce at all, and then the Scriptures would be honored and no problem of any sort arise. But it seems that people aren't like that. They make mistakes in picking out marriage partners and then they wish to be free of them. If the church stands fast on the Scriptures it cannot abide either the divorce or any subsequent remarriage. But if the church is to love one another, and forgive one another, how can it censure one another at the same time?

That's what the study was all about, and indeed it seems that three years were only enough to uncover the magnitude of the problems, much less provide answers. The couple involved—let's call them George and Anne—never did hear anything definitive about their profound dilemma, but the church grew to appreciate the complexities involved with applying the perfect will of God to His errant children.

Near the end of the first year, the committee came up with a rather frustrating report. Nineteen pages were involved and the conclusion left a lot to be desired:

"This paper is presented with a considerable degree of frustration. Due to the fact that there was no general unanimity of agreement, one is left with an uneasy feeling. Perhaps there should be no clear pronouncements of position on the question. It is obvious that individual churches will take action, as is already being done in various places, as seems best to meet the needs of a specific case. Thus the responsibility of making the relevant decision rests with the congregation."

If the committee experienced "a considerable degree of frustration" it can well be imagined what the betrothed George and Anne must have experienced. The report hardly satisfied their request for a definitive answer to their problem.

But in fairness to the committee it should be realized that their task was difficult, if not simply impossible. One absolute—God's Word—was being questioned, and mere men were to come up with another absolute to answer the question. If the committee had pronounced, "You must not marry; God is against it," the couple could reply, "But God is love. He would not condemn us." If the committee pronounced on the other hand, "You may marry after all; times have changed and the church must take a redemptive view of your situation," doubtless some within the church would object to undermining the authority of the Scriptures. They would say, "Then we may all sin as we see fit and expect that God will wink at our behavior. What will be the end of such easy license?"

The church, at least at that point in its deliberations, seemed unable to state a position for or against the remarriage of George and Anne. If they sanctioned it, they violated the letter; if they prohibited it they violated the spirit. Should the church condemn the remarriage, to the misery of its own members, or should it allow the remarriage, and appear to sanction what is pronounced to be sin within the body?

The committee dug in for further study.

And George and Anne got married.

New reports and new findings issued forth from the committee's labors as the three-year study went on. Searching for historical precedents, the examiners reached all the way back to Martin Luther and the beginning of the Reformation.

Luther held, according to a committee report, that marriage was "a worldly thing" and not sacramental in nature. The Roman Catholic Church of course held to the latter view and Luther was often in strict opposition to that church. Luther's position seemed to lead to civil marriages (and civil divorces) for Protestants. There was a noticeable softening of the letter of the law in regard to the grounds for divorce. "Malicious desertion" was added to adultery as a legitimate reason for divorce, and later on desertion came to include the refusal of "conjugal duty." Obviously, just the process the church now feared most—the steady eroding of the scriptural authority—had already happened in the past.

(We could follow this ongoing line of easier and easier grounds for divorce right up to the present where, depending on what church in what village we look at, we can find greatly simplified reasons for breaking the marital union. "Cruel and inhuman treatment" is generally a euphemism for a husband with a bad temper. "Incompatibility" normally expresses the fact that the couple weren't able to achieve what they considered to be a satisfactory sex life together. It is common in divorces today for a couple to ask an attorney which will be the most convenient grounds to utilize in their particular case to assure a speedy and comfortable divorce. Obviously the scriptural admonitions are of no consequence whatever in many churches today and the worst fears of those who warn against any adulteration of the biblical position have been realized.)

The committee found in their historical research that the Anabaptists, to whom the modern Mennonites trace their roots, did not go along with Luther's views of civil marriage and divorce, but held that "the marriage bond has always been valued as a mystical association and form of piety." This placed them somewhere between the Roman Catholic image of marriage as sacramental and the much looser "Protestant state-church interference," as they characterized it.

The Anabaptists thus took marriage more seriously than Luther's followers, but they were not so clear regarding remarriage. The committee studied carefully the Wismer Resolutions of 1554, which stated, "In case of deliberate adultery, the innocent party may be free to remarry after consulting with the congregation." Further investigation of the tendencies of congregations of those days in considering various remarriage cases led the committee to the conclusion, "The Anabaptists did not agree on whether divorced members were to be free to remarry. . . ."

We can imagine, from today's perspective, cases in which church members were profoundly disappointed with life under such rulings. Suppose a case of adultery breaking up a marriage and the church holding, for whatever reason, that neither partner could remarry. There would be one soul seemingly unjustly injured (the party innocent of the adultery). But, we can picture too that if the church invariably condoned remarriage for the innocent party, there might well be many nasty cases of church investigations into the habits of those claiming innocence. We can imagine a witch-hunt atmosphere as contesting parties in divorces let accusations fly out of malice. We can well suppose that the congregations found it easier to disallow all remarriage and be done with such infighting.

According to the committee's findings, though, no solid position on remarriage was established. And the struggle goes on today.

Looking diligently at the attitude of their denomination in more modern times the committee noted that "in the first half of the twentieth century there evolved an almost unanimous position that divorce and remarriage *under all conditions is sin,* and that no remarried divorcee or person married to a divorcee could remain in the married state and be received into the church while the former companion is still living." That kind of position probably simplified a great deal of arguing in the church, but it also opened a Pandora's box of troubles associated with the forgiveness of sin.

Jesus came to forgive sins, He said. He told His disciples, "Truly, I say to you, all sins will be forgiven the sons of men, and whatever blasphemies they utter" (Mark 3:28). Couldn't the divorced people, or the divorced-and-remarried people say, "Just a moment. I'm a Christian and my sins are forgiven. Aren't we all sinners anyway? Why put me out of the church for *this* particular sin?"

And true enough, congregations still differ in their regard of how serious a sin divorce and remarriage is. Some groups tend to receive divorced people into the church and some not. The committee had not discovered, to that point in their studies, a cut-and-dried position that everybody subscribed to in practice, however the various views were stated in theory.

One can almost picture George and Anne stepping down the aisle at one moment in the committee's deliberations, and being called back at another. Their frustration with the lengthy investigation must have been supreme.

The committee did not take at face value the early twentieth-century view stated above but sought further light along the lines of forgiveness of sin. One of their reports dealt with "forgive-

85

ness and acceptance upon confession of sin," and stated, "This position assumes that divorce and remarriage can be forgiven like any other sin, and that when persons have been divorced and remarried in ignorance and unbelief, they can find forgiveness upon confession of this and other sins. It holds that they can be received into the church in whatever state they are and that no effort needs to be made to try to untangle their marital involvements of the past. . . ." The statement concluded, "Proponents of this view cite the following statement of Paul, 'Every one should remain in the state in which he was called' (1 Corinthians 7:20. Verse 27 goes on, 'Are you bound to a wife? Do not seek to be free. Are you free from a wife? Do not seek marriage.) The application of this Scripture in such cases is also questioned by some," the committee reported.

The committee studied a conclusion reached in a ten-page study by another church leader. The author pondered the Lord's statement regarding "what God hath joined together" in an effort to reach a true, scriptural definition of marriage. "It would seem that this statement," he said, "is fulfilled when accountable persons voluntarily become one flesh by sexual union. Impracticable as this answer may be, I am unable to find a different answer in the Scripture."

The author held that adultery finishes a marriage: "Both Mosaic legislation and the exceptive clause of Matthew show that adultery severs the marriage union."

So the maxim of the law, at least for that investigator has to do with sexual intercourse. It begins a marriage and must be kept exclusive to it. Should sexual intercourse occur outside of the marriage the marriage bond is severed. Sex is the beginning and the end—the hallmark of when a marriage begins to exist and when it terminates.

Apparently thinking along the lines of putting the rightful sexual partners back together, the committee considered briefly whether divorced and remarried persons should dissolve their present unions and seek to return to the first husband or wife, but this idea was discarded as being nonscriptural. Such action was called an "abomination before the Lord" (Deuteronomy 24:3, 4) and is not "suggested in the New Testament."

One can well imagine the troubles there! What good result could come from an abundance of new divorces for the purpose of seeking to reinstate old marriages. This approach would seem to compound the problem rather than solve it.

The committee, when all was said and done, never did give a definitive answer to the request of George and Anne, and indeed there may be none. Perhaps the committee showed that the question has no answer after all. Perhaps once people get divorced they will never again be able to conform exactly to Scripture on these matters.

But it cannot have failed to occur to God that His children would make mistakes, would sin, and would twist and turn to carve out the best possible lives for themselves on earth. Most parents are quite able to predict their own children's shortcomings, and God is no exception. He many times provided for the sins of individual men, and His master plan of redemption for the mass of mankind obviously speaks of a Creator without delusions about His creatures. God knows men and God knows sin.

So what *is* His will in the matters of divorce and remarriage? Is there a way to apply sound biblical principles to up-to-date problems?

The committee, with all its arduous application to the divorce-remarriage question, found only that the problem has been historically difficult, and that Christians throughout the centuries have wrestled with it without real success. But is there a practical theology of divorce and remarriage adaptable to today's situations and still faithful to Scripture?

Researcher Martin uncovered further study of this challenging area by Professor Paul M. Miller of Associated Mennonite Biblical Seminaries, Elkhart, Indiana. Miller teaches Practical Theology, appropriately enough. He has carefully studied marriage, divorce, and remarriage, examining all that Scripture has to say on this area that may be pertinent to the modern condition.

Few Christians are unaware that divorce is a bigger problem in the church today than ever before, and more than a few fear some future personal involvement with this issue.

We turn now to Miller's views on divorce and remarriage as presented to a group he served as resource person, and to their responses in the form of some pretty hard questions.

5
One Man's Practical Theology

Professor Miller's remarks were not exactly for Christian beginners. A fairly thorough knowledge of Scripture and Christian ethics in general was assumed, and Miller addressed himself to the subtler considerations of the divorce-remarriage question.

We do not submit Miller's thoughts as definitive, of course, but they do represent an up-to-date Mennonite effort to deal with the problem by an informed spokesman. In the next chapter we will review the practical theology of another thinker with another approach. We submit the following, then, in the spirit of an inquiry, hoping that it sheds some light into some dark corners, as has been our purpose right along.

Miller began his lecture by giving a picture of the climate Jesus encountered when He addressed Himself to marriage and divorce. He had to contend with the reactions of His own disciples, as well as with the views of the Pharisees, which had developed through millennia under the Mosaic law. To find common ground, Jesus referred all the way back to Genesis and the first marriage, while utilizing His own life and spirit to illustrate the profundity of God's views on the union of man and woman in marriage.

In Matthew 19, Miller pointed out, Jesus dealt very broadly with the entire field of male-female relations, even touching upon celibacy as a valid way to serve God and the coming kingdom. Jesus also dealt with Moses, and of course with the gravity of the divorce situation. He seemed to harden the criteria for divorce, specifying only adultery as grounds.

When some Pharisees sought to test Jesus' views specifically on grounds for divorce by asking, "Is it lawful to divorce one's wife for any cause?" (Matthew 19:3), Jesus directed their minds back to creation. "Have you not read that he who made them from the beginning made them male and female, and said, 'For this reason a man shall leave his father and mother and be joined to his wife, and the two shall become one flesh'? So they are no longer two but one. What therefore God has joined together, let no man put asunder" (Matthew 19:4-6).

God began by creating Adam, Miller went on, and mankind was "him." When Eve was added, mankind became "them," but the "them" was of course still traceable back to the image of God. The "them-ness" became "joined-ness" as the first marriage was accomplished, and the new oneness of the marriage still reflected the image of God. The model perfected in Adam was carried through to Eve and to their new relationship. God is manifested and honored in the first marriage. The first marriage was the joining together of two versions of God's own image, and thus became a kind of third version. The marriage was God manifested, just as Adam was and Eve was.

God's image goes on and on in mankind, through the generations and millennia, and through the millions of marriages which combine God's creatures. He is still manifested today, and we still honor that original model when we yield to the demands and mutuality that is marriage. Even in modern times, marriage "continues" God's image. It never diminishes, but continually varies.

So Jesus is really saying that the miraculous autonomy (that is, one human creature made by God) is preserved in marriage. A new oneness occurs where the autonomy is preserved and two independent creatures combine with no loss of that original model's characteristics. It's rather like lighting one candle from another; the original loses no light and two are each as bright as the one was.

The marriage union restores a profound oneness between man and woman just as there was before woman was created from man. They *were* one, and marriage makes them one *again*. Thus Jesus was saying to the Pharisees, "How can you break apart what God had originally constituted as inseparable? If the Father said the two are one, why do you even look for possibilities of pulling them apart?"

Jesus clearly recognized that marital union did not in any way detract from the full image of God possessed by each human being. Each man and woman brings to their union the image of God and they continue to yield themselves to God together. They each have their separate autonomy before God, but are divinely created so that they can combine their autonomies in mutuality.

This, then, is our ideal: to consecrate this new union—this marriage—to manifest the image of God as fully as did each single person before the marriage.

"The coming together of man and woman," Miller said, "achieves the same oneness that Adam possessed before Eve was taken from his side. Those of you who know home, marriage, and love, pulling together, and sex union, know that there are mystical moments when virtually separate identities seem to fade into just one person. This mystery—this strange experience of oneness coming out of two—is what Jesus held out as perfect marriage."

As to divorce, Miller went on, Jesus held to the strictest spirit of the Torah, the first five books of the Bible which comprise the law. He stated firmly that God intended *no divorce* to begin with. Men's hearts were hard, however, and a compassionate Moses gave reluctant divorce specifications. But Jesus' first preference is clear: God's will does not include divorce, with the exception of adultery, which we can now see demolishes the wonderful and exclusive union that marriage is intended to be.

Now the Pharisees had in mind a long list of grounds for divorce that they and their ancestors had encountered and utilized through the ages.

92

It ranged from proven infidelity on down to bad cooking, we suppose, and they wanted to present their whole list to test Jesus' particular position in reference to it. They got nowhere that way: Jesus stayed with adultery as the only grounds. He said, in effect, "Your whole list is beside the point. All that you think you've uncovered in the foibles of human behavior—all your eagerness to find good reasons for discontinuing marriages— don't mean a thing. The fact is, God doesn't have any such list. God doesn't know any good reasons, other than that I have specified, for divorce. So you can put your list away and get back to the Torah!"

But Christ's own disciples seemed a bit taken aback by this uncompromising stand. "If this is the situation between husband and wife, it's better not to marry," they observed (Matthew 19:10).

The disciples seemed to be saying that if marriage were going to be so demanding and so vital to God that it could never be dissolved except by sin, it might be more circumspect to do without it. After all, marriage seemed awesome if its dissolution were to be a sin like murder. They would prefer to have nothing to do with it in that case. Why make such a difficult investment if you can do without? Perhaps the disciples would have been more comfortable with Moses' concessions than with Jesus' hard line.

But the Lord, who had so many times reminded His followers that "with God all things are possible," reassured them. Were they not believers? Had they not accepted the Son of God and were they not awaiting His kingdom on earth? Did they imagine that God had created for them an impossible choice? In Matthew 19:12 Jesus makes clear that His disciples will be fully able to accept His pronouncements on marriage and divorce, and He goes on to say that even "some people will be able to accept eunuchhood. Some are eunuchs because they are born that way," he told them. "Others are made that way by men. Still others have renounced marriage because of the kingdom of heaven." Obviously the disciples had not begun to imagine what they could achieve walking with God.

If a normal man can come to prefer celibacy (eunuchhood) in order to serve the kingdom, certainly another man can put up with one marriage throughout his life. If God can grant to some a life of no marital relations whatever, He can surely grant to others the patience to live within the bounds of one marriage.

And the Lord, of course, was a standing example of one committed completely to the will of His Father and taking no interest in marriage, though His human body functioned as other men's (He grew tired, hungry, He wept, and the like). The implication was clearly that service to God, for some, was gratifying far beyond the satisfaction of their desires for sex and marriage. So fully can the Father call and inspire His children that they can readily forgo thoughts of their own fulfillment in favor of His calling and His mission.

In brief, the disciples said, "We can't" and the Lord said, "Sure you can!"

Jesus spoke in revolutionary terms: there was a

new kind of life force available in the world, *His* life force. Those sharing in it would have heretofore unknown reserves of spiritual power with which to confront life and its problems. Those committed to the Christian ideal need have no fear of other commitments, like marriage for life. Those dedicated to Christ could also be dedicated to marriage, and would no more renounce the one than the other. They would, Jesus told His disciples, be able to accept this and triumph. Jesus' followers would never have to back out of anything, including marriage.

The ancient Jews had grown accustomed to loopholes in the law, Miller explained, as with the divorce loopholes permitted by Moses (Deuteronomy 24:1). But Jesus promised that His movement would have no such need of loopholes. Instead, power would be available for the fulfilling of commitments by even the least confident of Christians. Followers of Christ would find themselves equal to life and its trials and temptations, and like their Master they would be victorious.

Miller pointed out that such a concept had not been developed before Jesus' time at all, and that the pronouncements of Matthew 19 had once and for all supplanted the exceptions of Deuteronomy 24. Something entirely new had entered the world.

Also entirely new was Jesus' fairness in dealing with men and women. The older law had become very chauvinistic in practice. *Men* were the ones who put woman away in divorce; *women* were the ones who were convicted of adultery. It was certainly a man's world, in which only men might terminate marriage and only women were considered impure in adultery. Jesus charged that a man who remarried after divorcing a wife was also guilty of adultery. The Lord came down heavily on the patriarchal temple thinkers when He stated that men were guilty of adultery when they merely *looked* at a woman with lust.

This was "really carving out new ground," according to the speaker, who specified that up to the time of Jesus there was a double standard in Israel. Men controlled the spiritual affairs of the nation; it was up to women merely to remain pure. Women could be stoned for adultery; for men it was more of a misdemeanor.

Jesus stretched the definition of adultery into new territory in Matthew 19:9, with the implication that adultery is not just confined to the area of sex. Defiance of the marital vow *in any form* constitutes adultery, He implied. But God does not appear to accord sex such ultimate importance as men do. God did not utilize sex in the creation of Adam or Eve or in the incarnation of Jesus, who was virgin-born. In heaven, the Scriptures indicate, there will be no sex or marriage. Thus if God did not choose to honor sex in creation, in the incarnation, or in heavenly places, the weight of Jesus' view of adultery (God's view, in effect) ought not to come down wholly on this man-centered activity.

There is, of course, much more to marriage than sex. And we do enter into more than the marriage bed when we take the vows of matrimony.

What is the true essence of marriage? According to Miller marriage demonstrates four separate actions: the sex union; the civil sanction, or marriage license granted by the state; the church blessing, involving the sacramental presence and witness of the praying church; and the vow undertaken by the two hearts. It is this last, the vow, that Jesus seemed to regard as the true essence of a marriage. And if that is true, then it is easy to see how the breaking of that vow constitutes the breaking of that marriage.

Adultery, it is easy to see, destroys marriages. It is an obvious violation of a basic promise. But in the sight of the Lord the exchanged vow of marriage until death is the real issue. Break *that* and everything is broken.

The marriage vow deletes every other person to whom the marriage partner must be faithful for life. It is utterly exclusive, concerning only the two partners and establishing their ongoing fidelity to each other and no one else. The mere lusting after another person outside the vow breaks it as certainly as actual sexual contact with that outsider, according to Jesus' ideal.

Thus "looking" might as well be adultery; it certainly contains the same devastation where the marriage vow is concerned.

The vow is the center of the marriage, and not sex. We might consider God's covenants with men: God makes the vow, and it is His vow which is the essence of the particular economy. The carrying out of the implications of the relationship (*e.g.*, men's sacrifices under the Mosaic covenant) are like sex is to marriage—they are part and parcel of the arrangement but not really the central issue of it. The shared promise is really the central issue.

To carry the example to its logical end, Israel obviously did not forever lose its chance to come to God by failing to carry out the sacrifices—the gospel came "to the Jew first." All of God's *promises* regarding the Messiah were fulfilled despite the infidelity of the Jews where the law was concerned. *But,* when the Jews fail to receive the *promises*—God's vow to them—then they reject the true essence of their marriage contract with God. When they fail to receive the Messiah, then truly they are divorced from God.

So, sex is not the main issue of marriage and the Lord did not confine His definition of adultery to sex, according to Miller. The Lord considered that the breaking of the marriage vow by *any* nonexclusive activity was tantamount to adultery.

To consider the new covenant, Christianity which Paul likens to a marriage relationship (Ephesians 5:31, 32), again the essence of the covenant lies in the promises, not in our performance of it. We are admonished to create good works in the name of the Lord, and to honor Him by leading sanctified lives. But we shall not reap the overwhelming rewards of Christianity because of good performances, but because God has promised them.

We shall go to be with the Lord even if we have stumbled in our Christian lives, as Peter and the others did. But we shall not go to the Lord if we do not believe His promises because this is a lack of faith. We must "believe in the Lord Jesus" in order to be saved (Acts 16:31).

A marriage boils down to this, according to Miller: God joins people together and sanctifies their union when the vow that they make to each other is absolute, total self-giving commitment to forsake all others on earth, and when this love is placed even above the love for parents. Hence, a man leaves his father and mother and is joined to his wife.

That vow, made in faith in God, allows God to join together a couple in what is virtually a new creation. The vow is the thing and the covenant is what God acts upon. The sex act man shares with the animal kingdom, but the creative ability to make a vow is man's alone. Characteristic of his Creator, man is able to make promises and keep them.

The vow goes on in marriage, we can see, even after sex has had its day. Many an aged couple find such delight in each other as to be the envy of the young people around them, and their sexual activities might have ceased long before. What they are enjoying is the fulfillments of their original vow of marriage. They have certainly held each other in the esteem and exclusivity that they originally promised before God, and God has honored their union. Sex was their delight for its season, but their vow goes on and on in its beauty and sanctity.

We mustn't sell sex short either, of course. It is the life stream through which God now does His new creating. He has given to men an enormous responsibility in creation, to say the least. We stumbling creatures have the power to create, or not create, numbers of new creatures. What an overwhelming commission!

Our first responsibility to the new creature, our child, is to bring him into a climate of love. Anyone who has ever raised a child is quite aware of how sensitive these little ones are to the quality of relationship between their parents. If the marriage vow is working right and has not been violated the child will enter into a love covenant supplied by and nurtured by God. If not, the child will enter a bleak existence indeed.

But it is every child's birthright to be born of a couple who have committed themselves to non-separation, at least. The child is not equipped to understand divorce and ought to *be able to expect* a secure noninterrupted upbringing.

Finally, it is obvious, Miller concluded, that making a new life and making the union that brought it into the world to begin with are much the same thing. God makes marriages; they are acts of God. And God then says, "Don't pull them apart. When I have put them together, don't let any man find cause to pull them apart again." The famous King James rendering "What therefore God hath joined together, let not man put asunder" has been utilized for situations from digging canals to surgery on the human body, but it correctly applies, as Jesus used it, to marriage. Man is not to think about taking apart what God has decided, for good reasons of His own, to put together.

As marriage is like life itself, pulling it apart is like killing it. Indeed adultery, Jesus' sole divorce ground, bore the same penalty as murder in Israel. We should thus take the position that to contemplate divorce is as wrong as to contemplate killing someone to resolve a difficult situation. People should be pleaded with to go to any lengths to work out a solution for a bad marriage short of divorce as strongly as we would appeal to them to lay down a loaded gun and talk instead of shooting.

And if they divorce anyway? Miller asked, in all fairness, what then? Well, we have a gospel of forgiveness for murderers and we have a gospel of forgiveness for adulterers. We can have forgiven murderers, like Saul of Tarsus (the Apostle Paul), sitting in our congregation, and honor them and love them and use them, and hear all that they have to say—if our forgiveness is just that broad. And we can have forgiven adulterers in our church. God's forgiveness is just that broad.

Now we don't solve the problem by making a marriage a light thing and divorce not a serious thing. The thing we do when we have to confront divorce is that we emphasize the awesome grace of God to forgive people and His readiness to accept those who have sinned back into His family.

We are sinners, every one of us, Miller said, wrapping up his lecture. If we say we're not the truth isn't in us, the Scripture declares. It doesn't make a lot of sense for us to pick a special sin or two to not forgive. That's not Christian.

Miller then invited questions from his audience and he didn't have to ask twice! Few

Christians are unconcerned about these particular issues.

We reproduce the questions and answers here as they were given, edited slightly for clarity.

Q. *There's one thing that bothers me. I know God can forgive a person who commits adultery, but does that make it all right for them to do it?*

A. Well, your question is really about an individual sinning willfully. It's one thing to say that we are a fellowship in which a forgiven murderer can be totally accepted—even to the point of becoming our teacher—and quite another thing to talk about willful sin. What about an individual who sins when he knows better?

Now there's no limit to the way God can use forgiven sinners. The Lord didn't hesitate to appoint Saul as an apostle. That's why I have hope that our people in the church will be willing to do a little more than the world ever demands before they give up on their marriages. But there's some pretty straight teaching in Romans about *calculated sinning.* "Are we to continue in sin that grace may abound?" Paul asks. And he answers his own question definitively, "By no means!" The Book of Romans forcefully warns us against doing wrong things deliberately, willingly, and then presuming that God will forgive us if we just ask Him.

Q. *Which is the essence of marriage: the vow made between the partners to be husband and wife or the sex act?*

A. I think what you're wanting to imply by

that question is, "What will violate my marriage and ruin it?" You may be thinking, "If the sex act is not really the essence of marriage, then adultery would not really ruin marriage. If a partner makes a mistake it can be forgotten; we married 'for better or for worse.' "

But I'm afraid that adultery thoroughly violates the marriage vow, and I think Christ makes that very clear. The surface definition of adultery is simply someone having sexual intercourse with someone other than his or her spouse. That's the dictionary definition, the rabbinical definition, the legal definition, and the Mosaic definition. But Jesus carved out a *second* definition. In Matthew 5 He says that anyone who looks lustfully at a woman commits adultery. Why? Because by that very looking, that lustful wanting of a woman other than his wife, he has already violated his heart commitment to his wife.

Jesus compared that lustful looking, that searching around for something more desirable, to the adultery he found in Israel when He accused the nation of wanting another God. Israel had a covenant but they failed to obey it; they looked elsewhere for satisfaction. "Adultery" and "idolatry" not only sound alike, but they are in essence the same thing. Both do violence to any agreement, whether between God and Israel, Christ and the church, or husband and wife.

°   °   °

Miller struck here on a most meaningful point for Old Testament readers. God did indeed describe Israel's apostasy as adultery, devoting

103

virtually the entire Book of Hosea to this single concept. C. I. Scofield's commentary on Hosea says, "Israel is Jehovah's adulterous wife, repudiated, but ultimately to be purified and restored. . . . Israel is not merely apostate and sinful—that is said also; but her sin takes its character from the exalted relationship into which she has been brought."

God Himself comments on Israel's irreverence and characterizes Himself as a wronged husband in Jeremiah 31:31, 32, when He announces the new covenant: "[It will not be] like the covenant which I made with their fathers when I took them by the hand to bring them out of the land of Egypt, my covenant which they broke, though I was their husband, says the Lord."

The questioner's intent, seemingly to separate sexual matters from the marriage vow, is not successful in view of clear biblical principles. Adultery broke the *vow* between God and Israel; it was not just another sin, but the sin that ruined the relationship. We may thus conclude that a nagging wife or a bossy husband does some harm to marriage, but an adulterous wife or husband utterly ruins it.

* * *

Q. I have a question about a trend that is current among the so-called "thinking young." They reword their marriage vows to eliminate the promises about chastity and sexual faithfulness to the partner. Their reasoning, while it may not have the blessing of the church, is that if they do not take the vow of sexual continence there will be no violation when they take on an outside sex partner later on.

A. Convenient, but Scanzoni says that the idea that you can disassociate sex from committed relationships is not working. He refers to some research done on call girls who tried to accomplish separating their work and their committed relationships; the research showed that these women disintegrated in about five years, which is about the maximum length of time a normal woman can hold together trying to disassociate her life dreams and her self-respect.

To me, it's very hard on married people in general if sexual fidelity is not a part of their mutual commitment. Everything within me and everything that I find in Scripture says it's wrong to treat sex casually, or to try to make a vow that goes, "It's you and me, except in sex."

Q. There's a clear distinction between fornication and adultery—sex, say, before marriage, and "outside sex" within marriage. How do you deal with that? Is there a clear-cut scriptural comment?

A. Recently I did some premarital counseling with a young couple who wanted to get their sex started well before they married. They said, "Look, we love each other, and since love is the essence of marriage we want to start having sex right now. Why not?"

So I asked the young fellow, whose beard was just starting to bloom, "Are you ready to take full responsibility for her? What if she were in an accident tonight and were crippled for life? Are you

105

ready to take on wheeling her around in a chair for the rest of your life? Are you *that* committed to her at this point?"

The young man hedged in his answer. All he could say was, "Well, we're not really going to be married for some time, you know. Her father is paying her bills now." He seemed to be telling me that if something awful happened the responsibility belonged to the girl's father.

I had to tell him, "Well, you want her to give herself to you totally, but you don't want to pick up a whole lot of responsibility for her. You don't mind the pleasures of her womanhood, but if she needs some real help her daddy will take over for you. You're not ready to stand up before society and say, 'I am totally responsible for her,' but you want her to be totally liable to you and your wants. I think that until you can say honestly that you're ready to take care of her for life, no matter what happens to her, you're just using her. You're just borrowing a part of her while somebody else is her real support."

I don't have to cite Scripture, I suppose, to show that fornication is as wrong as adultery. People who have never seen a Bible can come up with that. You're really asking me about human nature and I have no delusions about it; people will do what they know is wrong.

But we're here to discuss what's right.

Q. Could you deal with my situation? I'm divorced. I have a little girl who says, "Mom, I sure hope you get married again. I want a daddy to live with us. Everybody else has a daddy." But if anyone married me now he would be living in adultery, right?

A.   You're referring to Matthew 5:32: "But I say to you that everyone who divorces his wife, except on the ground of unchastity, makes her an adulteress; and whoever marries a divorced woman commits adultery."

Well, I think the Lord's intention here was to get after that male chauvinist society that said a man could get divorced but a woman couldn't. The men in His time were divorcing their wives "on the side" so to speak. Now to look carefully at Jesus' choice of words in the original Greek, we find a passive verb; we might render His statement about a man divorcing his wife as ". . . causes her to be committed an adulteress." This is a slightly different feeling. The Lord may have been indicating that that particular society would automatically tend to blame a divorced woman of adultery. They would tend to assume, maybe for convenience or male chauvinism, that the woman was at fault for the divorce and that she must have committed adultery. The divorce would cause an innocent woman, perhaps, "to be committed an adulteress."

We get more meaning when we consider the society Jesus operated in. They were awfully tough on women. When a woman was accused of adultery they brought her to the Lord and asked if they should stone her, as if she alone had committed the crime. They simply let the man go, although he was obviously culpable. The woman was stoned, plain and simple, and that was the end of the matter.

Now to a society like that one you have to talk very realistically, and draw them a clear picture. "You will cause your poor wife to be considered an adulteress," He was telling those men. "She will be shamed. Anyone who marries her later on will be automatically marrying an adulteress. She'll be permanently branded. Think about *that*!"

Now to get back to your situation, I think *our* society is different today than that of Jesus' time. I don't think people around you brand you an adulteress because you were divorced. They *do* put a brand of some sort on you, each according to his own thinking about divorce, I guess, but few people today automatically assume that divorce is invariably caused by adultery.

But I still think that I'd rather back up one notch and say, "Let's try to save your marriage, even in its present shape, despite the divorce," than tell you to go out and remarry, whatever society thinks. I just think that the whole people of God have not done all they can and should do to preserve marriages. I don't think Matthew 5:32 is the last verse we should work with on this problem; I think more can be done by people who have the mind of Christ.

I'm just asking that if you as a Christian, and the whole church around you, could do all that you are capable of in Christ, couldn't you save your marriage? Couldn't we all preserve more marriages and not have to fall back on what the precise laws about divorce have to say?

We have a solid strain of teaching which we could draw on to say to you that you are not called an adulteress by us. We don't call you guilty of adultery because you're divorced. We offer you forgiveness and acceptance like Jesus did. On the other hand, I'm a marriage counselor and a firm believer in the idea that there are no innocent parties in marital problems. That's just how life goes.

But this is important—if your divorce was forced on you by the other party, then we approach you as innocent. We help you bear your burden.

Frankly, the remarriage question is a lengthy and difficult problem usually best taken up in individual cases. As you can see I'm not completely aware of your specific situation. I can only outline general principles in this setting, and hope to clarify some murky issues. I hope what I've said gives you something more to go on than you had when you came today. That's all I can say for now.

* * *

Miller was on the spot in that foregoing question. We can certainly agree that the remarriage question is a tough one and an individual one. It's a little like the abortion question—it would seldom come up if everyone adhered to God's teaching in the first place.

People seek abortions because they made a mistake. They didn't want the child they initially took a chance on conceiving. In the vast majority of cases some good idea of God's was discarded— unmarried people had intercourse, or an adulterous marriage partner took a gamble outside the marriage. People also want *divorces* because they made a mistake. They didn't, after all, want the marriage they initially promised to uphold. They want to break the vow they declared was unbreakable.

If a basic law of God is broken there is obviously going to be some confusion down the line. People shouldn't have intercourse so casually that weeks later they want to undo the consequences. People shouldn't marry who are unable to keep a vow.

Easily said.

But people make mistakes. That's what the gospel is all about.

°　°　°

Q.　I think the church in general might be too dedicated to the vow concept, even though it's a valid idea. Surely it's the vow that makes the marriage what it is, but what about couples who have stayed together after their vows have been broken, and lived in a "hell-on-earth" situation?
A.　Well, I agree that the vow can be broken while the couple is living together, and that makes things pretty rough.

Q.　Okay, should these people whose vow is broken continue to have sex together? I mean, isn't sex defined as total self-giving, and isn't it an awful hypocrisy to go on with this self-giving once the vow is broken? Isn't it a little hard on the integrity for people to live together and play at marriage just because divorce is too terrible to contemplate?

A. All right, I understand. You're bringing up a case that does happen in the church. There are people living together who are doing so just because they don't want to get a divorce. They have sex, or they don't, as they choose, but anyway they keep up a pretense of marriage.

Well, I think separation is a possible solution there, and it's not forbidden in any way. Paul talks about it in 1 Corinthians 7 and he says that if one partner wants to leave then he should go ahead. I'm certainly not lauding separation as a solution to marital problems; I'm just giving you the biblical commentary. But if you bring up the hypocrisy of fake marriages then I have to fall back on the solution in the Word.

Much better of course would be for the people in the marriage, who once presumably really loved each other, to quit faking and get at their problems in prayer and faith. Faced with only separation as the biblical solution, surely the Christian should be inspired to seek answers to the problem. I have seen more than a few real restorations of "hopeless" marital situations.

o   o   o

Miller might here have brought up the example of God and Israel again. The Book of Hosea does not show God giving up on His adulterous wife but restoring her. The new covenant, after all, was made with Israel (Jeremiah 31:31, 33). God will have solved the vast problem of union with the chosen people at the end of this age when "all Israel will be saved" (Romans 11:26).

It could be argued that God Himself has undergone a separation from His adulterous wife in this church age. A remnant of Israel does come to the Messiah in each generation, but God has announced and carried forth His plan to give the Messiah to the Gentiles. The separation will have a happy ending at the return of the Lord, when the adultery will have been forgiven and forgotten (Zechariah 13), and Israel accepts her King.

◦   ◦   ◦

Q. About 25 years ago people from Pennsylvania went down into the Appalachians to do missionary work. But when they tried to enforce the marriage and remarriage rules of our church it hurt them. The hill people just weren't able to live with the restrictions.

A. Well, on the other hand, "open marriage" isn't too successful either. There's a trend toward the "old-fashioned" kind of strict monogamy coming out of the World Council of Churches in Geneva, Switzerland. The Council conducted a three-country sociological survey which showed that people are getting pretty tired of this "living together without commitment" thing. The whole business of disassociating sex and marriage is just a romantic, teenager's dream at this point. And I hardly have to mention that it has no basis in Scripture.

People don't like rules, but they don't like anarchy either.

◦   ◦   ◦

After fielding some additional questions,

Miller finished the session beautifully with the following remarks:

I have enough childlike faith to believe that people caught in the divorce situation can be helped through prayer. The effectual, fervent prayers of the righteous can be focused upon them and they can be counseled. I think some stories could be changed if we were all to unite in the prayer, "Lord, what wilt Thou have me to do?"

You see, I do not believe in the old romantic notion that love operates only when marriages are formed—"Oh, I'm caught up. . .I love this person. . .I'm helpless.'. .I've got to get married." Love is much more than that. Love is learned. I believe two people can learn to love as they start caring, making sacrifices, doing things for each other, even if they have to grit their teeth at first.

You know, that's the way mothers learn to love babies. After a while they really love them—those little creatures that fill their diapers so regularly and make for nothing but hard work. I believe that married couples who have lost the track of love can find it again. Love grows out of devotion and sacrifice, and I'd like to see troubled couples really have a go at those things. It takes time and effort, but look at the time and effort we'd save in trying to work out these problems.

We should all devote ourselves all the time to plain old love, the kind that builds over the years, that slowly invests and waits to collect interest.

That finally is the real answer to all of our questions.

6
Another Man's Practical Theology

Theologian-Counselor Howard H. Charles, also of Associated Mennonite Biblical Seminaries, Elkhart, Indiana, one day addressed the very same topics as his colleague Paul M. Miller had. Actually they join thousands of thinkers going back virtually to the days of the Lord's very pronouncements in examining the marriage, divorce, and remarriage quandary.

We consider Howard Charles' thinking now, not in the spirit of showing where he differs from Paul Miller but in the spirit of more inquiry. Actually the two theologians come out very much the same, given the difficulty of their subject, and their slight contrasts simply provide more information for us.

The setting was a little different for the following section; Howard Charles held forth in a local Mennonite Church and his remarks were all of a piece—actually a message to the church. A question-answer period was involved, but the time was given more to the professor's conclusions and analyses about Scripture than to the individual queries of the listeners. Norma Martin audited the session.

The professor's point of departure was strictly

the Bible, rather than the social realities of the present day. He dealt mainly with the admonitions and counsel of the Lord rather than concentrating on the problems of the church. His opening remarks set the tone: "I'm glad to be part of a brotherhood that takes the Bible seriously as a guide for faith and life, and that takes the congregation seriously as the place where Bible study is done and decisions affecting faith and conduct are made. I'm pleased to learn how you have been involved as a congregation in the matter of trying to ascertain what God's will is on this question of divorce and remarriage."

Howard Charles got directly to the heart of the matter in his talk, going to the gospel passages we discussed earlier: Mark 10:2-12, Luke 16:18, Matthew 19:19, 5:31-32. The four passages, when placed side by side, the professor suggested, say four important things about the question of divorce and remarriage.

First, the husband who divorces his wife, except for unchastity, makes her an adulteress. Second, a man who marries a divorced woman commits adultery. Third, a woman who divorces her husband and then remarries commits adultery. Fourth, a man who divorces his wife, except for unchastity, and then remarries commits adultery. To boil those down to a simpler statement, if there was no adultery present in a marriage in the first place and a divorce occurs, neither the man nor the woman may remarry without incurring adultery.

But life is not so simple, apparently. People, including Bible believing, sincerely faithful people, somehow divorce and remarry. An increasing number of Christians have incurred this sin of adultery through divorce and remarriage.

Howard Charles is not unaware of that situation and did not end his talk with a statement of the rules and regulations.

Some questions obviously arise in connection with the four Gospel statements. Howard Charles first dealt with the nagging query, "Just how does a man make his wife an adulteress if he divorces her?" After all, what if she never did commit adultery at all? What if he just didn't love her anymore? What if he just got tired of her? How does *she* end up holding the sin bag?

Howard Charles differed somewhat from Paul Miller's analysis of this difficult Scripture in the preceding chapter. "The answer," Charles said, "is that if a man divorces his wife for reasons other than adultery, he places her in a position where she is likely to contract another marriage. And since the first marriage was broken up for reasons other than adultery, it is still biblically regarded as valid. The husband therefore forces his wife into adultery by making a situation wherein she is likely to remarry when in principle the first marriage is still regarded as valid."

The famous "exception" clause—"except for unfaithfulness" (or unchastity, etc., depending on the translation)—of Matthew 19:9 has probably caused many sleepless nights and raises hard questions by itself. What is "unfaithfulness"? How does this exception relate to the general rule itself? How potent an exception is it? How do we reconcile this exception clause, found in both Matthew 19:9 and Matthew 5:32, with the absolute prohibitions on divorce found in Mark and Luke? Those latter Gospel statements present no such exception to the prohibition against divorce.

Translations from the Greek original have helped somewhat to define the term "unfaithfulness" as it is used in the exception clause. The Greek term can mean a variety of things, all related, such as fornication, incest, sodomy, and adultery, according to Howard Charles. The meaning of the term in a given instance depends on the context in which it is used, he explained.

The context in the Matthew passages is the marriage relationship. Jesus is talking about marriage, and unfaithfulness here likely means adultery, most modern students agree. Howard Charles and a great number of other scholars hold that what Jesus was saying in Matthew's exception clause is that a man who divorces his wife for reasons other than adultery commits that same sin if he remarries.

In reference to the exception clause—how it relates to the remainder of the statement in which it is used—does it apply only to divorce, the first part of the statement, or to remarriage as well? Howard Charles believes that the exception applies to the total statement—the Greek syntax dictates that where adultery has been committed, there is not only the possibility of divorce, but also of remarriage for the "innocent" spouse. There would be no sin involved in remarriage if the original divorce was caused by adultery.

As to reconciling Matthew's exception clause with the absolute prohibitions in Mark and Luke, Howard Charles admitted it gives theologians some difficulty. There are those who think that the Matthew exception was actually made by the church; they feel that Jesus' original teaching is found in Mark and Luke, and the exception was inserted. The church, they feel, tried to soften a situation too hard to live with. They made an escape clause.

But most conservative scholars feel that the exception is genuine. How do they reconcile the exception statement in one Gospel with the absolute prohibition in two others? Howard Charles says, "The absolute statements give us Jesus' *general* teaching, which is in principle, *no divorce*. Matthew, however, gives us a more *precise* statement, formulated with a view to a *particular* situation— the case where adultery has been committed. Here divorce with the feasibility of remarriage is an option." He also pointed out that the thrust in these two Matthew passages is not on the exception clause as such but on the prohibition of divorce on all other grounds.

Since many arguments have been advanced for each of these positions, Howard Charles suggests a somewhat different approach. He proposes that the exception clause, whether it was made by Jesus or by the church, be not considered as arbitrary regardless of *who* made it. The professor says further that he is inclined to think that it was Jesus who authored the exception clause, and that if He did, He "did not begin by admitting that the absolute prohibition of divorce was a very high and difficult standard."

Howard Charles doesn't think that Jesus decided that He may have gone a little too far and then decided to relax things a bit. If He arbitrarily settled on adultery as the only exception, then Jesus might just as well have picked on some other sin.

By making adultery the sole exception, the professor says, Jesus revealed a realistic understanding of the nature of this sin and its effect upon the marriage relationship. "Marriage, at heart," Howard Charles said, "is a life-long mutual covenant between one man and one woman, in which each gives himself/herself wholly and exclusively to the other—body, mind, and spirit. This exclusive self-giving in mutual love finds its highest expression and most intimate symbol in sexual intercourse."

Howard Charles quite appropriately points out that adultery strikes a blow at the very heart of the marriage relationship and shatters the inner meaning of that relationship. To be sure, adultery is more likely to occur where a marriage is inwardly already dead or dying. Nonetheless, the overt act of adultery represents a sort of ultimate step in the breakdown of the relationship. It is this desperate situation that is envisioned in the teaching about the relationship of adultery to divorce. On the other hand, he cautions, this doesn't mean that when one's spouse has been found in adultery he or she should "rush off the next morning to the divorce courts and dissolve the marriage legally." He adds that not only does formal divorce not necessarily have to follow the commission of adultery, but in many cases actually does not. He urges penance, confession, forgiveness, and renewal of the covenant in order to restore inner substance and integrity to a marriage shaken by adultery. He does concede, however, that "adultery by its very nature strikes a mortal blow at the heart of the marriage relationship."

The third problem raised by these four statements mentioned earlier, he says, has to do with the question of whether adultery is a state or an act. "According to Jesus," he says, "adultery is committed when remarriage follows divorce for reasons other than adultery.

"In such a case," he asks, "is the adultery that is committed in a remarriage an act or a state?" Howard Charles says that if it is a state, a second marriage can never be valid as long as a former partner lives. Breaking up the second marriage, he adds, is the only way to deal with the sin of adultery in this situation.

The situation can be viewed differently, he says, if "the sin of adultery is regarded as an act committed against the first marriage at the time when the second is inaugurated and shattering its meaning as argued above." In such a case the divorce and remarriage is indeed to be considered sinful. But Howard Charles offers comforting words when he says: "When that sin has been taken care of through genuine penitence and the experience of forgiveness, the second marriage need not be dissolved but may continue as a valid one."

The professor strongly cautions that "whether adultery is an act or a state is a very crucial consideration in the matter of how you deal with a remarriage where the preceding divorce was for reasons other than adultery."

Charles admits that the New Testament is not so clear on this matter as we would like. He wishes that it offered a precise and clear answer as to whether adultery is an act or whether it is a state. He feels that since the New Testament does not speak directly to the issue, "we must try to put things together as best we can."

The professor reasons that if the exception clause was not made arbitrarily, but realistically dealt with the shattering effect of adultery upon the marriage relationship, then it appears that this particular sin is an act. "You can't keep on shattering something that is already shattered. You can't destroy something which no longer exists."

He thinks that Paul did not regard adultery as a state. From what we know of the Corinthians it is very likely that many of these Christians must have had divorce and remarriage in their pre-Christian background. If Paul had regarded divorce as a state he would have counseled taking steps to terminate the second or perhaps fifth marriage." The professor admits that this is an argument from silence and that not too much can be based on it. To bolster this line of reasoning, he notes that the phrase "living in adultery" does not occur in the New Testament.

He feels that Paul's most important passage dealing with divorce is 1 Corinthians 7 where he deals with two different situations. The first is that of two Corinthians who can't seem to make their marriage work. Paul says if they decide to separate they should remain unmarried or they should be reconciled. Remarriage is not an option for them. The second situation is the case of a mixed marriage where one spouse has become a Christian and the other remains a pagan. Paul says the Christian should not take the initiative to break up the marriage if the unbeliever wishes to continue in the marriage relationship. If, however, the unbeliever wishes to terminate the marriage then the Christian "is not bound" to prevent it from happening or to force the unwilling non-Christian to continue living with him or her.

Howard Charles says that by his use of the phrase "is not bound," Paul may refer to more than the obligation to continue the marriage. He may be adding a second ground to that found in the teaching of Jesus on which divorce and remarriage can take place, namely, desertion. If by his use of the phrase Paul means that the deserted Christian is free to contract a new marriage such would be the case. Again a footnote from Paul would be helpful.

The professor concludes from his studies of the teachings of Jesus and those of Paul that the Christian does *not* have the right to take the initiative in terminating a marriage. He must work for its redemption and preservation. "But what does one do," he asks, "where in spite of all personal efforts of friends or of a congregation, a marriage does break up?"

In such a case, Charles says the Christian ought not to be the first person to rush off to find another mate. He feels that if a Christian really wants to take the New Testament seriously, he needs to keep the door for reconciliation open as long as possible. This normally would mean until it is closed by the remarriage or death of the former spouse. The burden of responsibility for working at the matter of reconciliation cannot be shifted from the shoulders of the person who wants to be sensitive to the teachings of the New Testament.

Charles does not think it would be wrong for the Christian to remarry if the former spouse remarries because then the door of reconciliation has been closed. But the Christian may prefer to keep open the option of the possibility of a remote future reconciliation. This, he says, is his or her privilege and if conscience dictates this course of action it should be followed.

Professor Charles poses this interesting question: "If divorce and remarriage for one reason or another does occur, is it a sin that prevents a person from ever again being or becoming a member in good standing in the Christian fellowship?" He says that Mennonites face two difficulties in seeking to answer this question. The first one grows out of the Mennonite heritage of strong emphasis upon Christian conduct. "This," he says, "leads easily to a type of moralism with the assumption, perhaps unconsciously held, that in order to be a good Christian our past record must be free of the blot of such a sin."

He says the second and closely related difficulty is the Mennonite "sluggishness" in grasping the radical character of Christian forgiveness as taught in the New Testament. "This," he says, "involves not only the matter of proper intellectual understanding but the even greater difficulty of internalizing the doctrine in our feelings and attitudes toward persons caught in such situations. We often have difficulty accepting persons into our fellowship even though they may give every evidence of having experienced God's forgiveness for their sin."

Professor Charles cautions that two points need constantly to be emphasized in Mennonite teaching and preaching. The first, he says, is that *all* divorce is sin. The professor states that it is a breakdown of God's intention for man, namely, that the marriage relationship should be terminated only by death. There is need, therefore, for confession and forgiveness whenever this occurs. He says the New Testament gives no license for conduct which is contrary to the will of God for us. Divorce occurs because of human sinfulness and should be recognized as such.

This fact, the professor says, leads to the second emphasis: "This is that where there is an honest facing of the situation in genuine penitence, the way is also open for the experience of the miracle of forgiveness. Where forgiveness truly occurs a new day has dawned with fresh possibilities for life both in relation to God and to others."

He cautions, however, this doesn't mean that where there has been confession and forgiveness there is no responsibility to the past. "Where there is the possibility of the reconstitution of the broken down marriage on a new basis, this is our Christian obligation," he says. "But where the door is closed to that possibility by the remarriage of the former spouse, permission for the contraction of a second marriage without guilt need not be withheld from such a person."

Professor Charles would add one final word. Although some of his interpretive procedures may appear to be overly concerned with formal considerations and to be almost legalistic, he would not wish to be so understood. Neither the teaching

125

of Jesus nor Paul on divorce and remarriage are full discussions of all aspects of the problem. They offer only a few broad and basic guidelines within which specific decisions will need to be made. They primarily set limits of action rather than expound the dynamic essence of a true marriage relationship. It is the latter which should be our major concern.

Is Howard Charles too strict or too lenient?

That's the sort of question that comes up, when all is said and done, about a theologian. The "too strict" folks will quote the professor as saying, "All divorce is sin," which the professor indeed said. The "too lenient" folks will opt for, "Permission for the contraction of a second marriage without guilt need not be withheld," which he also said.

If all divorce is sin, how can there be any sort of permission for a second marriage without guilt?

That question is answered in the gospel, of course, as well as by the professor. It has to do with the radical character of Christian forgiveness. Christian forgiveness vanquishes sin and guilt; properly applied for, with due repentance, it is totally effective. If it is not totally effective the fault must be with the condemner, not the sinner.

With all of his exactitude in examining the Scriptures, and with all of his "hard line" statements— and Howard Charles is not namby-pamby about the gospel—the speaker concluded, as we all must finally conclude, that "the way is open for the experience of the miracle of forgiveness."

Howard Charles and Paul Miller agree, and the two seem to agree with the Lord. The Christian life never reaches a truly hopeless impasse—not for the thief on the cross and not for the divorcee. There's room at the cross for everyone and the Lord has provided cleansing for any sin we can imagine. Leprosy was the concern of our Lord, and blindness; and He said we would do even greater things than He did by way of healing and the other miracles.

It is our Christian obligation to reconcile marriages, even when a divorce has broken them, says Howard Charles. But it is our Christian obligation also, he says, to extend the grand forgiveness of the gospel. "Where forgiveness truly occurs a new day has dawned."

Of course, practically speaking, if there were less sin there would be less of a forgiveness problem. If there were no divorce, there would be no remarriage question to analyze. If there were no adultery, marriage in general would be a more positive undertaking.

To that end Norma sought out people who were willing to talk about sin—and particularly the sin of adultery. Potential adulterers are not hard to find; the whole human race is involved. But potential adulterers who are willing to speculate about their own adultery possibilities are something else again!

Norma found some. They were realistic and candid churchgoing, God-fearing men who knew their own weaknesses and were seeking some preventive medicine. They were willing to sit down with their pastor and take apart the adultery question, not in theory but as a very real possibility in their own lives.

They were willing to go on record, and the next chapter is devoted to their honesty.

7
Accidents Waiting To Happen

Some people—Christians included—consider adultery an accident waiting to happen. They dread the day when they might get caught up in this constantly lurking temptation, and those who speak out candidly often admit to nagging doubts about their own virtue under pressure.

Adultery, the marriage killer, must be the most "honored" of sins; the church has always tended to regard it as especially dastardly and perhaps the most perverse of backsliding possibilities. Somehow we forgive almost anything before we forgive adultery.

Thus Pastor Ray Bair and the Belmont Mennonite Church, or at least the men of that church and one woman who contributed to the discussion, sought to confront this thorny sin. Frankness was the keynote of the investigation into adultery, and nobody seemed to hold back. Norma Martin has reproduced the proceedings.

The discussion, needless to say, was sober and biblical. There was no trace of snickering at such a topic and all present were respectful of the candor displayed in the church. If a viable "solution" for adultery—a way of handling this temptation—could be found, doubtless much marital suffering would be averted. If, among the many persons present, someone had discovered a real way out, everyone would certainly be interested.

But the gathered faithful were all still in the flesh and few expected a breakthrough.

Pastor Bair's biblical perspective seemed broader, at least at this gathering, than Paul Miller's or Howard Charles'. He drew upon Scripture from Isaiah to Revelation in establishing the concept of Christian holiness, in departure from the usual concentration on the gospel admonitions. On the other hand, his group was addressing a more far-reaching topic than simply the problem of divorce and remarriage. Adultery, like music and war, is common to all people.

Pastor Bair set the tone of the discussion by defining holiness, which he finds comes in two basic varieties. To begin with, there is the holiness imputed to us by God when we receive Jesus Christ and the Holy Spirit into our lives. Then there is the holiness progressively achieved in this life as the Christian yields himself to the Holy Spirit. There is, in effect, an automatic holiness that becomes ours because Christ provided it, and there is a second level of holiness that we can achieve by walking in the Spirit according to the Lord's commands.

The pastor demonstrated the first kind of holiness, the gift of God, by referring to 1 Thessalonians 4 and 2 Corinthians 5; the latter makes clear that God "made him to be sin who knew no sin, so that in him we might become the righteousness of God."

"But there is also a second level of holiness the Bible talks about," Bair said, "and that is the kind of holiness into which we grow as Christians. This is the practical, actual holiness achieved as the Christian yields himself to the Holy Spirit. It is an imperfect but progressing holiness and righteousness—one that is always growing to perfection."

He next referred the congregation to Hebrews 12:14-16 and 13:4. "Strive for peace with all men, and for the holiness without which no one will see the Lord. See to it . . . that no one be immoral. . . . Let marriage be held in honor among all, and let the marriage bed be undefiled; for God will judge the immoral and adulterous."

Pastor Bair interpreted these passages this way: "The writer is telling us to make an effort on this thing. This is part of our Christian discipline to strive for deeper, greater holiness in life. This practical holiness is not going to be given to us automatically. Rather, this daily growth in holiness comes as a result of continual striving to achieve the goal. Holiness is a major concern in the Scriptures. You know, the Bible includes a good deal about holiness.

"If you will turn to Revelation 22:11 and 15," he said, "you will notice that the closing theme is the second coming of Jesus. Verse 11 says, 'Let the evildoer still do evil, and the filthy still be filthy, and the righteous still do right, and the holy still be holy.'

"And notice in verse 15: 'Outside are the dogs and sorcerers and fornicators and murderers and idolaters, and every one who loves and practices falsehood.'

"Now look back to Revelation 21:6-8 where it says, 'It is done! I am the Alpha and the Omega, the beginning and the end. To the thirsty I will give water without price from the fountain of the water of life. He who conquers shall have this heritage, and I will be his God and he shall be my son. But as for the cowardly, the faithless, the polluted, as for murderers, fornicators, sorcerers, idolaters, and all liars, their lot shall be in the lake that burns with fire and brimstone, which is the second death.'

"Then," Pastor Bair continued, "over in chapter 20, verse 13, it says, "the sea gave up the dead in it, Death and Hades gave up the dead in them, and all were judged by what they had done.'

"This is the description of the way the dead are to be judged," he said. "You notice it says judged by what they had done! Judgment will be on the level of practical holiness; some way our works are woven into the judgment structure. In the passage in 1 Thessalonians 3:13 notice that Paul said, 'So that he [that is the Lord] may establish your hearts unblamable in holiness before our God and Father, at the coming of our Lord Jesus with all his saints.'

"Now you can go through the Scriptures again and again, and the matter of holiness, the matter of righteousness, of cleanliness of life is brought to us as a major issue. I'd like to underscore, then, that God wants holiness within. You notice that was brought out in verse 13. It is God's will that we should be holy. Probably the most tremendous worship scene pictured in the Old Testament is Isaiah 6—that chapter where the great affirmation is made, 'Holy, holy, holy is the Lord of hosts!' "

Pastor Bair related that God is holy, and that the

Scriptures tell us that if we are to become holy like Him, we must become holy within. "Jesus' words concerning adultery in Matthew 5," he said, "clearly indicate, first of all, that holiness is an inner condition. In that passage Jesus says that adultery is a matter of lusting; an inner desire become rampant, uncontrolled.

"In other words," he continued, "Jesus is saying that the inner desires and lustful thoughts of the uncontrolled mind are tantamount to adultery."

Bair pointed out that while lustful thoughts do not have the same immediate evil effect as an overt act toward breaking down a relationship, they do just that in God's eyes. The inner heart and not the overt act is what sets up the actual condition of sin. The sinful act itself is only the outward manifestation of the inner condition of the heart.

"None of us here," Pastor Bair continued, "myself included, have never lusted in our hearts. We have all indulged in this form of perverted love—which is all that lust amounts to. But we sin when we allow these thoughts to linger in our minds and do not seek to control them by prayer. Instead of asking Jesus to remove them, we indulge in pleasurable fantasy. And thus we lust."

Bair clarified his thoughts about lust by pointing out that there is a difference between sin and temptation. He admitted that because of the permissive society in which we live it is particularly difficult to avoid lustful thoughts. But these tempting thoughts only become sinful, or lustful, he said, when we "cuddle" them in our minds. It is then that we must ask God for forgiveness so that we may be made clean, or whole again in Jesus.

David's remorseful cry to God after his adultery with Bathsheba illustrates God's concern with an inner cleanliness, or holiness of the heart, according to Bair. David's appeal to God was for Him to create in the errant king a clean heart. "He didn't say, 'God, make it so that I won't commit adultery again.' I think David knew where that sin had started. It hadn't started in his eyesight. It hadn't started with the physical coming of Bathsheba to him. That sin had started from an inner condition that had somehow grown cold, lax, and careless enough so that David allowed his lustful thoughts to dwell within his mind.

"Perhaps he couldn't have avoided seeing her in her bath," Bair continued, "but he could have turned away and asked God to remove his sinful thoughts. When that kind of cry comes from an earnest desire, God will perform His miracle of cleansing our thoughts and bringing us that inner holiness."

When Pastor Bair opened the meeting to discussion from the congregation some interesting and revealing methods of resisting extramarital temptations were unfolded. While the meeting was intended primarily to elicit information from the men, one young unmarried woman offered her thoughts on "reverse male chauvinism," with men, rather than women, being the "sex objects."

The first man to speak up used a business trip to the West Coast, with a stopover in Chicago, to explain his feelings on the subject of temptation in general.

Being all too familiar with the loneliness that

businessmen encounter on extended trips from home, he said he decided to have his wife accompany him. Their plans called for her to join him in Chicago, where he had to attend a board meeting of his company, prior to proceeding together to the Coast. He said that the meeting had been rather hectic and that he was looking forward to a relaxing few hours at the airport before taking off for the second part of the trip. Unfortunately his wife was unable to locate their continuation tickets from Chicago to California. Getting reticketed consumed in a frantic manner all the time that he had looked forward to for "unwinding" from his morning meeting.

The important client that he flew out to call on met them at the airport. This time, instead of plane tickets, his wife couldn't find their luggage claim stubs. He said that although he did manage to maintain his composure before the important client, his anger was very real. That night before retiring, instead of having a loving discussion about the day's unfortunate incidents, as was their custom, they went to bed with angry criticisms and retorts running through their minds.

He awoke at 3:00 a.m. (jet lag factor), and lay in bed wondering why he had brought his wife along on the trip. He thought about the several offers of "companionship" for the night that he had received from women in his Chicago hotel. When he and his wife had started arguing about the previous day's experiences, he was absolutely certain that from now on he would travel alone. Furthermore, he had convinced himself that there was no need for him, or any other traveling man, to spend the night alone in a hotel room. "Companionship" was there to be had, after all, and without all the hassles caused by a wife on the scene. He would just give in to adultery on the next trip, and who would know the difference?

"But then," he said, "a providential thought crossed my mind. I remembered an article in a national magazine I had recently read predicting the number of marriages and divorces for the coming year. This article estimated that there would be four million marriages and two million divorces. Then it went on to discuss the heartbreak of not only the man and woman in each divorce, but of the children, the expenses involved, and the difficulty of trying to establish a new identity.

"Those thoughts jolted me back to reality," he continued. "I guess it made me realize how really unimportant the lost tickets were. Anyway, when I looked at the alternatives, I thought my wife and I should talk the whole situation over."

He said that his wife confessed that she had been nervous about meeting a lot of his business associates who were strangers to her. She told him that her apprehension had caused her to misplace the tickets. In turn, he admitted that he had wanted to make a good impression on his important client, and he had felt that her carelessness had put him in a bad light.

"The upshot of it all was that we decided to pray together that morning," he added, "and I guess that was the most meaningful prayer of our entire life together. It was really worthwhile," he concluded, "and all I want to say is that when all else fails, turn to prayer."

"Well," Pastor Bair said, "that pretty well sums up what I said earlier about the difference between temptation and sin. Just because the Lord allows these thoughts to enter our minds doesn't mean that we have to submit to Satan. There's nothing out of the ordinary for us to have these thoughts. It's simply a matter of what we do with them after they're there."

The next congregation member to approach the microphone described briefly the culture, or subculture, as he called it, in which he was raised. He said that common-law relationships rather than Christian marriages were the rule. He said these situations were unstable and both the partners, and children born of the "marriages," were emotionally harmed.

"I'm appreciative of what the church teaches with regard to marriage," he said. "I'm also gratefully learning what it means to be a husband and father to my wife and children.

"I think that my wife and children," he added, "are the promises spoken of in the Scripture which says, 'Seek first his kingdom and his righteousness, and all these things shall be yours as well.' I don't think that God could have done a better thing for me. Adultery cannot deliver what God provides."

A woman spoke to the group next, in a rare facing up to feminine lust. Unless she's in a class by herself, women also are tempted in much the same way as men.

"Well, I'm not married, and I'm not a man (sorry about that)," said the only woman participant in the discussion. "But I just can't sit still for this poking and prodding any longer. I think the Lord is prompting me to say something.

"For the last—oh, I don't know how long it's been," she continued, "we've been hearing about women's lib and about how men have been treating women as sex objects. But during the past several weeks I've come to realize that I'm doing the same thing with men—except in a little more subtle way.

"You know," she added, "we think that if a man is handsome or attractive, he's supposed to be sexy, or—I don't know just how to put this, but I know that sometimes when I'm walking down the street and the guys drive by in their cars and whistle or give me some comment, I really get mad. I think it's kind of insulting, but then I sometimes look at a man and say to myself, 'Wow! He's really neat.' It doesn't really come to your mind, but you sort of know—it's just there. You don't really admit to yourself that that's what you're thinking, but that *is* what you're thinking. I suppose that if I could whistle, I'd whistle at some of the men I see! And I guess that's adultery of the heart, as Jesus put it.

"And I don't know what to do about temptation," she concluded, "but with the Lord's help I'm trying to change my way of thinking. I mean I'm trying to think of men as other human beings, and not necessarily as mere sexual objects. I just don't want illicit sex in my life."

Another man turned to Paul's instructions to women in Ephesians and Colossians in which the apostle told them to be obedient to their husbands, and for the husbands to love and show kindness to their wives.

"I've always wondered why he talked about the men needing to love their wives. He never talked to women about that. Evidently they were loving their husbands okay. It's we men who have the problem of loving, so I guess that's why we were the ones to whom he addressed himself.

"My wife and I have been reflecting recently on what it means to really love someone," he continued. "We think we have pretty well interpreted the passages in Ephesians and also the one in Genesis about a man leaving his father and mother and cleaving to his wife—or something like that. I never got an "A" for memorization.

"But I think we've misinterpreted what it means to cleave," he continued. "Many times I think we *clutch*, and many times I think we smother each other.

"You remember that some months back we heard a woman who is a leading authority on relationships. She said that when we become married, the two really become three. She said we are still separate people and that we have to maintain that individuality without smothering it in the other person. Together then, we do become a distinct third person without eliminating the existence of the two individuals.

"If that's true, then adultery is unthinkable. It would be that third individual splitting himself in half, so to speak, and sneaking off from his other half.

"I just want to read a little thing that a friend of mine wrote," he continued, "and that I think speaks to the whole issue of what I would call smothering love in a marriage relationship. And I

139

think I have been just as guilty of this as anyone else here.

   "I want to love you without clutching,
   To appreciate you without judging,
   To join you without invading,
   To invite you without demanding,
   To leave you without guilt,
   To criticize you without blaming,
   To help you without insulting,
   If I can have the same from you,
   Then we can truly meet and enrich each other.

   "That says a lot about where I am now and how I have to be more respectful of my wife," he continued, "and also more respectful of each of you as Christian brothers and sisters.

   "The other thing I would like to say is that my wife and I have found over the years, and more particularly in recent years, the real importance of the brotherhood in helping us love each other in appropriate ways.

   "I think," he concluded, "that my wife and I are unable to work through the normal hassles of any relationship on our own. And I think that's one of the things that we, as Christians, need to put into our interpretation of Matthew 18. I mean that our marriages need to come under the lordship of Christ and the discipling process of the church, as well as our individual pilgrimage with the Lord."

Once the participants warmed up to their discussion, their subjects began to range over far wider, and sometimes surprising areas. The next speaker brought up the human tendency to pout whenever displeased by his mate—a rather subtle, but sometimes quite painful manner of making the other suffer for some real or imagined wrong committed. Nonverbal disapproval can be devastating.

This man revealed how he had pouted at some length that very morning because his wife had criticized him for shoveling the snow from only one side of the driveway when she thought he should have cleared both sides. He said his feelings were hurt because he felt he had really done an adequate job, and that her criticism about his being too lazy to clear off both sides hurt his manly pride.

He reported that after a half-hour or so of his "silent treatment," she went to him and asked what his problem was. He admitted that then he "felt on top of the situation" because he had made her come to him. Other times, he reported, the roles were reversed.

He readily pointed out that this was one of his many childish games husbands and wives play with each other. And, he added, games indulged in too often can lead to rather drastic results in a marriage. There are many pressures in marriage not found in adultery. Adultery is easy compared to marriage. If the marital game-playing gets too nerve-racking, there's a real danger of adultery coming up in the mind as a solution.

When discussion from the floor ended, Ray Bair returned to specific biblical passages to fortify the godly requirements for chastity and marital fidelity.

He pointed out that the Matthew 5 passage

clearly states that adultery is not just an outward act but also pertains to the inner condition of the heart. He said that when Paul referred to sexual immorality he also included the spiritual and personal immorality so carefully described in the Scriptures.

"Sexual purity," Bair said, "is not just a physical thing, but it means keeping oneself pure for the covenanted person, whether that person be God or a mortal being.

"Furthermore," he continued, "whether we are immoral or not is not determined just by a physical act, but by the known effects of that act, either upon our relationship with Jesus Christ Himself, or, if we are married, upon our beloved one."

He also said that if an act in itself is an innocent thing, but is harming the marriage, it becomes immoral. "It is not just a matter of actions," he continued, "either good or bad in isolation, but the effect it has on building or destroying a covenant relationship.

"Another thing I would like to point out is that purity of body calls for disciplined control. The Bible clearly points out that a man's body is not his own. Jesus said that your body is a temple of the Holy Spirit."

"First Corinthians says that the wife's body belongs to the husband, and the husband's body belongs to the wife. As a Christian husband, my body belongs first to God and second to my wife. It is not mine to use or abuse as I may wish."

He admitted that the materialistic world in which we live today makes it difficult for us to live the holy and honorable life that Paul so often spoke of. "We are so accustomed to the materialistic philosophy of 'I'll get what I want when I want it,' that we can easily carry this over into our marriage relationship." The greatest safeguard for Christian marriages is to maintain intact the holy relationship we have with God. This godly relationship is equally important to single people. While God promises specific, definite punishment for those who reject His discipline, He also provides strength and power to maintain this discipline for those who accept it.

Pastor Bair addressed the wives of the men who were present. He told them that those women who live, act, dress, and think holy lives have a powerful influence upon their men. He said he did not think they were fully aware of the very positive influence these actions had upon their husbands, and he wanted to pay tribute to them.

"I don't think I can stress too much the tremendous effect that a wife's loving care can have upon her husband," he stated.

In his closing remarks Bair said that he thinks God has provided each of us with a conscience to help us to lead the holy life called for in the Scriptures.

"Now the conscience is not the Holy Spirit," he said, "and it is not easy to explain where one ends and the other begins. There are a lot of different ideas about the relationship of the two which I won't go into here. But I think the conscience is a mechanism God put into us. I believe that if we will respect it and let God use it the way He wishes, then it will serve its purpose well by being a tremendous safeguard for us.

"But," he cautioned, "we must be careful not to

override it, neglect it, or push it aside until its usefulness disappears. We must respect the fact that God has put a conscience within us to help us live up to our present level of understanding the difference between right and wrong.

"God is not schizophrenic," Pastor Bair continued, "but when God comes into our lives by faith, we receive the Father, the Son, and the Holy Spirit. Three persons in one. I won't try to explain it, but when He comes, the Father, the Son, and the Holy Spirit live within us.

"You know," he continued, "the question is whether or not we are allowing Him to fill us, to use us, to bless and control us."

Bair concluded, "So, you have everything when you have Christ, and you are filled with God through your union with Christ. God gives us His Holy Spirit to provide the strength to set us free in Jesus Christ.

"If we are trusting in Christ, His Spirit within lets us yield ourselves to the influence, the drives, and the controls of that Holy Spirit so that our lives may be pure, and that in a growing way we may be clean and holy even like our Lord."

Did Pastor Bair and the congregation solve the problem of adultery in the foregoing discussion? Are all our troubles over?

No, not really. Actually, few expected a breakthrough about adultery in this particular meeting. The church sought only to examine the problem. They wanted some light.

And that they got.

"Unfortunately," Ray Bair is a godly man. He

144

referred his flock only to the Word of God. He was not able to say, "Here it is—a way you can enjoy adultery and still be loved by God and your neighbors." And he was not able to say, "Here is a pill you can take which will quiet your adulterous desires. Now don't forget to take your pill."

The light the pastor was able to shed was the same old light we've always had, "unfortunately." We have the same Bible God gave us millennia ago, and we have the same consciences He provided us. We're the same bunch of sinners He originally arranged to save.

There probably *is* no breakthrough to be found concerning adultery. Plainly and simply, it's a sin, and sins aren't good for people. The net conclusion of the church after hearing the stories of those willing to participate in the discussion, and after hearing the adept scriptural analyses of the pastor, amounted to "go, and sin no more." Jesus gave the adulteress He encountered the same breakthrough.

Granted, people are very complicated and they seek subtle answers to human problems. There's nothing at all wrong with delving into the Scriptures in search of some solution modern folks can live with.

But in this instance it can be seen that there is nothing new under the sun about sin. Pastor Bair's concept of second level of holiness, a sanctified walk in the Holy Spirit, is thoroughly biblical and is done violence by adultery. Christians, and unbelievers too, do better without living lives of deception.

Bair brought up the matter of the human

conscience. We all have one, whatever we believe. "God has put a conscience within us," the pastor said, "to help us live up to our present level of understanding the difference between right and wrong." If unbelievers cannot live comfortably with a bad conscience, how shall the believers, who are responsible to God for their actions, accomplish this?

There are people with seared, nonfunctioning consciences. Psychiatrists work with people every day who have abused their own values to the degree that they malfunction mentally. Their consciences don't work anymore. Pastor Bair said, "We must be careful not to override [our conscience], neglect it, or push it aside until its usefulness disappears."

"That same old song and dance." If the reader expected either a comfortable way into adultery or a comfortable way out of it, this isn't the book, and Pastor Bair's church isn't the church. So far as the investigation of adultery went, it found no solution beyond what God has already said. We may ask more and more questions, but we already have our answer.

8
A CHRISTIAN LOVE STORY
By Zola Levitt

For anyone who has ever loved, the New Testament has a very special message:

> In my Father's house are many rooms. . . . I go to prepare a place for you. . . . I will come again and will take you to myself, that where I am you may be also. John 14:2, 3.

God is love, He says, and the heartening messages of the ministry of His beloved Son have many times been compared to a love letter. But really, the Word of Jesus Christ is more than a love letter; it is a proposal of marriage.

The church, the body of Christians, is the Bride of Christ, and the Lord came to make a marriage covenant with us long ago. Since His return to His Father's house we have waited in hope for that great day of the rapture, when the Lord Himself "shall descend from heaven with a shout" and take His bride. John the apostle sings, "Let us rejoice and exult and give him the glory, for the marriage of the Lamb has come, and his Bride has made herself ready" (Revelation 19:7).

147

This is hard to understand, literally. Paul wrote, "This is a great mystery," concerning the coming marriage of the Savior and His church.

But the mystery becomes more understandable when we consider the marriage customs of Jesus' people, the Jews. We who participate in the modern Western marriage culture fail to see the full significance of the actions of the Lord in regard to His marriage proposal. Jesus was drawing an analogy from the Old Testament Jews and their ways of matrimony, which reached back to the giving of the law. In that He was "sent only to the lost sheep of the house of Israel," and ministered primarily to the Jews, the Lord utilized the Jewish tradition to demonstrate this mystery.

In biblical times, the Jewish way of matrimony was not so simple as it is today (though some Jews today practice the ancient tradition). In the old days the prospective bridegroom would initiate the marriage by going from his father's house to the home of his bride to determine the price he would have to pay for her. He would pay the price there at the bride's home and then drink a cup of wine with her. This would establish that the marriage covenant had been made.

From the moment of the establishment of the covenant the groom and the bride were regarded as husband and wife. His bride was considered to be consecrated and set apart from society until the groom should claim her. A special betrothal benediction was said over the wine, indicating that a sacred contract had been made.

The groom would then return to his father's house to prepare a place for his bride. Separated for twelve months, the bride and groom would each make their special preparations for the coming wedding. The bride would gather her trousseau and the groom would work on a special bridal chamber in which the marriage would be consummated.

When the preparation period was done the groom would come for the bride, along with a party of escorts. The party would leave from the groom's father's house at a time chosen by the groom's father, and go in a procession to claim the bride. The bride knew, of course, that the groom was coming at the end of the period of separation but she did not know the exact time of his coming. Thus, the groom's arrival would be preceded by a shout from the escort.

When the bride would hear the shout she would know that her time for preparations was over. Her year of waiting in sanctity for the arrival of her groom was done at that moment and she had to be ready.

The bride, and an assembly of her female attendants, would join the groom and his party and the procession would go back to the groom's father's house. There they would find that a great many wedding guests had assembled. The wedding guests might know who the bride was but they could not see her face at this point because she was veiled. The bride and groom would be escorted at once to the bridal chamber and there they would consummate the marriage.

The friends of the groom and the bridesmaids

would wait outside the chamber until the groom came out to announce the consummation of the marriage. These close friends would pass the good news along to the wedding guests, who would then feast and make merry for the next seven days.

The bride remained hidden in the chamber for the seven days, along with her new husband, while the merrymaking went on. But at the conclusion of the seven days the two would come out, and now the bride would have her veil removed so that all could see who she was.

The bride was now married to her husband and would go with him to live in his own house.

Now we can better appreciate the work of the Lord in connection with the mystery of His coming marriage to the church. We are now the bride and are waiting for our Groom to appear to claim us.

He came to us first from His Father's house. He ascertained at our home, the world, that a dear price would indeed have to be paid for His bride (Luke 22:39-44), drunk a cup of wine with us to establish His covenant of marriage to us, and He fully realized (as He stated, "This cup is my blood") that the price for His bride was very high (Matthew 26:27, 28). But He drank the cup. Our covenant is given in Jeremiah 31:31-34.

As He left for His Father's house soon after, He promised to prepare a place for us and to return for us to consummate the marriage. We realized from His many entreaties that we were now set apart to await our groom and be sanctified. We were consecrated completely now to become this Groom's Bride at His next coming. We were, and are, "engaged," in modern terms, and we are entreated to act accordingly.

There has now been a long separation during which our bridegroom is preparing our place, but we have much to do. Our "trousseau" of good works must be assembled, and we must prepare for our unique married life to come.

At some future moment, known only to the Groom's Father, He will come for us, with an angelic escort. We will hear a shout (1 Thessalonians 4:16) and we will know that our waiting-in-hope is over. We know now that we have to be ready to go.

Our own wedding party, the past believers, will go with us and our Groom and His party to His Father's house, heaven. We will see a great many Old Testament saints assembled there who have gone on to the Father long before us but who will be excitedly awaiting our arrival and the wedding.

We will go at once into our Groom's bridal chamber and there He will know our secrets (2 Corinthians 5:10). Nothing will be hidden from the Groom in the chambers as we consummate our marriage (1 Corinthians 3:11-15). As we will have new bodies (1 Corinthians 15:51, 52) of a spiritual kind, our marriage consummation will be of a spiritual nature. We labored so that "we may be accepted of Him" and we need have no fear in the bridal chamber.

The friends of the Groom standing outside the chamber will not all know us when we arrive, but they will rejoice with the Groom as He announces the consummation. John the Baptist explained, "He who has the bride is the bridegroom; the friend of the bridegroom, who stands and hears him, rejoices greatly at the bridegroom's voice; therefore this joy of mine is now full" (John 3:29). How delighted John will be at that future moment when the Lord Himself has removed our veil!

The feasting will begin then, as the entire assembly of wedding guests gets the good news. The church has married the Lord! What a wedding announcement!

We will remain with the Lord for seven years, symbolizing the seven days spent by the bride and groom in the old tradition, and then we will come forth unveiled. The saints in heaven, and the whole world as we return with the Lord, will then see us and know just who the bride of Christ was! Many around us do not know us, or appreciate our position now; but when we come forth with the Lord unveiled, all will see us in our fullest glory (Revelation 19:7,8).

We will then live with our Husband in His kingdom.

Viewed in that context, marriage itself becomes quite a greater thing, and divorce and remarriage become grotesque. If marriage on earth between God's children is supposed to emulate the marriage of the King Himself, then we are dealing with a more serious, more godly, more precious human undertaking than we usually estimate.

Coauthor Levitt, accustomed to viewing Christianity from the Jewish perspective, finds in marriage one of God's most mystical establishments. The Apostle Paul, also accustomed to viewing Christianity from the Jewish perspective, spoke eloquently on marriage in Ephesians 5:31, (quoting Genesis 2:24), saying: "For this reason a man shall leave his father and mother and be joined to his wife, and the two shall become one flesh." And Paul went on to write, "This mystery is a profound one, and I am saying that it refers to Christ and the church" (v. 32).

If our earthly marriages are really models of that great marriage of the Lord Himself, then terminating them by divorce is as unthinkable as denouncing the Lord. We may as well tell the Lord that we refuse to accept His bride price—that we want to break our engagement—as to divorce our earthly spouse. If this perspective of the gospel is persuasive, then marriage is a very serious, very binding agreement held precious by God Himself.

Divorce, viewed in this context, becomes like refusing one's gift of salvation—handing it back to God, as it were.

But, of course, none of us is as yet married to Christ, nor to anyone so perfect as He. We *do* have problems with marriage, and some of us *do* get divorces. We began this book with the touching testimonies of some Christian people who did not discover another way out. We found their questions hard to answer, and their situations begged Christian compassion.

What does the Lord do when a Christian hands

back his salvation? Can a Christian who knows the Lord say, "I don't know Him"?

Peter did that.

Peter, under extreme duress, repeated three times over that he didn't know the Lord. Was he handing back his salvation? Was he saying, "I don't want to take part in this marriage after all," or "I want to get a divorce under these hard circumstances!"?

Whatever Peter was thinking, he stands as a prime example of the Lord's forgiveness. Peter repented and some seven weeks after his heinous lies he preached a sermon that saved 3,000 people! (Acts 2). The Lord continued to use Peter in spite of his earlier sin.

Howard Charles aptly described in chapter 6 the "sluggishness" among Christians to grasp New Testament forgiveness—the kind Peter received. "We often have difficulty accepting persons into our fellowship even though they may give every evidence of having experienced God's forgiveness for their sin," to repeat the professor's point.

This "Jewish perspective" toward marriage, and toward the sin of Peter and many others, says two things that seem like opposites: (1) we must not sin and (2) we must forgive sin. Those two things sound reasonable enough, but applying them to divorce and remarriage somehow becomes difficult for many of us. We find ourselves too many times condemning sin in the church, especially divorce, and yet we all, ourselves, sin.

We said earlier that we do not have the whole answer to the divorce-remarriage question. This would be a remarkable book if it ended with an answer to this complex problem. But we set out to shed some light into a dark corner, and we hope we have accomplished that. Through presenting actual cases (with names and details changed to protect the parties involved) and through the careful teaching of experienced scholars and counselors, we hope we have contributed to a compassionate and proper response to the difficult dilemma of divorce.

Norma Martin teaches in the Nursing Education Department at Lutheran Hospital, Fort Wayne, Indiana. She serves on the executive committee of Mennonite Nurses' Association and as editor of their publication, *The Christian Nurse*. She is also active in the Indiana Nurses' Association and the American Nurses' Association.

Her writing has appeared in *The Nurses' Lamp, The Lamplighter, Gospel Herald, Church and Home, Christian Living, Gospel Evangel, Mennonite Weekly Review, Mennonite Reporter*, and *Mennonite Life*.

Norma was born at Hanover, Pennsylvania. She graduated from Eastern Mennonite High School, Harrisonburg, Virginia; received her nursing diploma from Lutheran Hospital School of Nursing, Fort Wayne, Indiana; completed her BS in nursing at Eastern Mennonite College, Harrisonburg, Virginia; and earned her master's degree in Education at Indiana University South Bend Campus.

Norma was employed as an adult education teacher (1969-1972) with Indiana Vocational Technical College and with the Elkhart, Indiana, Community School System. She taught nursing education at Eastern Mennonite College in 1972-73.

She attends First Mennonite Church on Saint Mary's Avenue in Fort Wayne, Indiana.

Zola Levitt is host of a daily talk show, *The Heart of the Matter,* on KPBC Radio, Dallas, Texas.

A dozen books carry Levitt's by-line, headed by the best-seller, *Satan in the Sanctuary* (with Thomas S. McCall) released by Moody Press and Bantam Books. Other Levitt books include *Corned Beef, Knishes, and Christ* (Tyndale House), *Jesus—The Jews Jew* (Creation House), *Israel in Agony* (Harvest House), *Guts, God, and the Superbowl* (Zondervan), and *Christ in the Country Club* (Herald Press).

Born in Pittsburgh, Pennsylvania, Levitt completed his BS degree in Music Education at Duquesne University in 1961, his MM in applied music (oboe) at Indiana University in 1963, and the course work for his PhD in conducting at Indiana in 1970. He has performed with the New Orleans and San Antonio Symphonies and with Glen Campbell Show Tours.

Since his conversion in 1971, Levitt is in demand for numerous church speaking engagements, retreats, home Bible studies, luncheons, and the like.

Levitt and his wife, Yvonne Patricia (Golden), are the parents of a son, Mark.